D125920Z

Profit-Focused Supplier Management

Profit-Focused Supplier Management

How to Identify Risks and Recognize Opportunities

Pirkko Östring

AMACOM

American Management Association

New York • Atlanta • Brussels • Buenos Aires • Chicago • London • Mexico City
San Francisco • Shanghai • Tokyo • Toronto • Washington, D.C.

658.72
O85p

JK
*Special discounts on bulk quantities of AMACOM books are
available to corporations, professional associations, and other
organizations. For details, contact Special Sales Department,
AMACOM, a division of American Management Association,
1601 Broadway, New York, NY 10019.
Tel.: 212-903-8316. Fax: 212-903-8083.
Web site: www.amacombooks.org*

This publication is designed to provide accurate and authoritative information in regard to the subject matter covered. It is sold with the
understanding that the publisher is not engaged in rendering legal,
accounting, or other professional service. If legal advice or other expert
assistance is required, the services of a competent professional person
should be sought.

Library of Congress Cataloging-in-Publication Data

Östring, Pirkko, 1960-
  Profit-focused supplier management : how to identify risks and
recognize opportunities / Pirkko Östring.
        p.   cm.
Includes bibliographical references and index.
  ISBN 0-8144-7187-0
  1. Industrial procurement—Management.   2. Purchasing—Management.   I.
Title.

  HD39.5.O843   2003
  658.7'2—dc21   2003006950

© 2004 Pirkko Östring
All rights reserved.
Printed in the United States of America.

This publication may not be reproduced, stored in a retrieval system, or transmitted in
whole or in part, in any form or by any means, electronic, mechanical, photocopying,
recording, or otherwise, without the prior written permission of AMACOM, a division of
American Management Association, 1601 Broadway, New York, NY 10019.

Printing number

10 9 8 7 6 5 4 3 2 1

Contents

University Libraries
Carnegie Mellon University
Pittsburgh PA 15213-3890

Preface

THIS BOOK CAN HELP YOU to find the most suitable suppliers for your company and to keep your business on a course of excellence. This book is also practical and suitable for nonfinancial people. The case studies of fictional business analyst Jill Turner describe realistic work situations that an analyst would encounter in the business world. By observing Jill's methods, the reader can develop his or her own operating procedures.

Although Jill and the companies she visits are fictitious, the examples in Chapter 7 are taken from existing companies, such as Sanmina-SCI Corporation, Intel Corporation, and Marconi PLC. The opinions of those companies are based on published materials, with the examples of possible conclusions drawn from that material.

Steering a business is like steering a boat. When analyzing your suppliers, you should evaluate how well the business has done and how well it will continue to do. The *Pommern,* an old sailing ship in Mariehamn, Åland, made me realize that the business world is like life at sea: On sunny days, any captain with a crew can steer the boat without any problems. But on stormy days, it takes a skilled captain with a good crew to navigate safely to the port—to their goal.

In the business world, all businesses more or less flourish in the up markets. It doesn't take excellence in the company's top management to keep the company afloat. During the down markets, only the best managers can keep their businesses alive.

On a ship, the captain sets the course and the skilled crew knows what to do. In business, the president of the company—with the assistance of his team—sets the course, and personnel must put the strategy into practice. In sourcing, your goal may be to find excellent suppliers. I hope this book helps you learn how to gain better insight into your suppliers.

Introduction

THIS BOOK CAN PROVIDE YOU with a new and valuable approach for analyzing suppliers. It can assist you in identifying a supplier's strengths and weaknesses, and it is practical and suitable for nonfinancial people. This book should motivate top management to uncover more information about its suppliers, enable purchasing managers to select better suppliers, and give business controllers a tool for limiting risks and improving their companies' financial standing.

This book is a comprehensive guide for:

- ❑ Providing knowledge about financial statements in a user-friendly format in supplier context
- ❑ Analyzing a supplier's business and financial strengths
- ❑ Providing valuable ideas on how suppliers should be analyzed by a company
- ❑ Challenging workers to improve their knowledge of their company's suppliers
- ❑ Providing a new perspective about a supplier by offering guidance in understanding the supplier's business

The book is organized into three parts. Part One explains the background and the reasons why it is important to analyze suppliers, starting from a general level and concluding with the individual supplier level.

Part Two comprises the concept of corporate analysis, including the qualitative and quantitative elements that constitute corporate analysis, comprehensive explanations of financial statements, and comparisons of different accounting standards.

Part Three provides concrete examples of analysis: (1) the tools, (2) examples of analyses, and (3) useful sources for quickly finding relevant information.

Chapter 1 discusses the changing nature of companies. It begins by addressing changes in the business environment that are the reason behind the analysis and ends with an explanation of those reasons: first to the supplier base management level and second to the supplier level. The chapter ends with a fictional case (Case 1) showing the importance of analyzing a supplier and finding its financial strengths.

In Chapter 2, the starting point for the analysis is revealed, allowing a process to be defined. The meaning of the relationship among risk, risk management, and supplier and credit risk are presented. The risk factors affecting the selection of a supplier are determined after grasping the basic knowledge of risk management and the relationship between suppliers. The classification of suppliers is made to help in identifying key suppliers and understanding which suppliers should be analyzed and why. At the end of the chapter, a fictional case (Case 2) about a small supplier overextending its capabilities illustrates the importance of analyzing suppliers.

Chapter 3 addresses the details of corporate analysis. The chapter uses detailed definitions to discuss the quantitative and qualitative elements of corporate analysis. It provides a background for the idea of analysis. Quantitative analysis is based on financial statements and shows the financial performance and financial strengths of a company. Qualitative analysis embraces all nonfinancial aspects of corporate analysis and provides a backdrop for the financial profile. The conclusions give the corporate analysis reader value-added information.

Chapter 4 explains financial statements by introducing the key data for quantitative analysis. Every part of the financial statement is presented in a similar manner and then divided into sections to provide a better understanding of the structure of the item.

Each element of the financial statement is presented, such as the balance sheet, and followed by definitions and key questions to help readers understand the possible clues for analysis. The subchapters end by coaching readers to recognize "the particularly noteworthy issues" in analyzing. Some of these items include:

❑ *Balance sheet*—The snapshot of assets and liabilities and company funds, divided into parts to provide a better understanding of the structure of a balance sheet.

❑ *Statements of income*—The link between opening and closing balance sheets and the detailed contents of statements of income.

❑ *Cash flow statement*—Provides information about all the company's investing and financing activities during the period. It reflects the company's ability to generate cash. The subchapter key ratios provide clear definitions and formulas for the most frequently used key ratios.

❑ *Forecast*—Based on the core information collected in the previous subchapters. Readers learn the interrelationship between the numbers in financial statements and the value-adding conclusions.

At the end of the chapter, the most common differences between GAAP (Generally Accepted Accounting Principles) and IFRS (International Financial Reporting Standards) accounting standards are explained. The financial reporting of the publicly listed and privately owned companies in the United States, United Kingdom, Japan, and Germany are presented. The chapter ends with a fictional case (Case 3) about a Western analyst visiting a Japanese supplier.

Key questions or key points at the end of every chapter are included to help readers focus on key issues when analyzing their suppliers. The most significant questions are marked with an asterisk and here the trends of the company and its peer group are important to follow.

In Chapter 5, qualitative factors are described and their meanings illustrated. The qualitative factors are studied individually and also grouped together (environment, company, and ownership) to facilitate the reader's understanding of the entire process. The subchapter "Environment" illustrates external factors such as country, market, competitors, customers, and suppliers. The subchapter "Company" provides ideas for analyzing the strategy, management, and history of the supplier. The subchapter "Ownership" presents the impacts on the ownership of the company. The chapter ends with four fictional cases that illustrate real-life situations when visiting and analyzing suppliers.

Chapter 6 presents templates for analysis. The templates, short analysis and corporate analysis, are based on practical work to test and find the most informative and user-friendly templates.

Chapter 7 leads readers to concrete analysis by presenting a short analysis and two corporate analyses. The short analysis is of a listed U.S.-based company (Sanmina-SCI). The corporate analyses are of a U.K.-based company (Marconi) and a U.S.-based company (Intel) and contain useful explanations. The example companies were selected from different countries to inspire readers to make their own analyses even when the suppliers are in different countries.

The appendix presents the final but very significant part of the process: information sources. It presents useful information sources and additional information.

In summary, the book covers reasons for analyzing a supplier, starting with the risk and significance of a supplier to defining a suitable method for analyzing the supplier, and the outcome of the suitability of the supplier for a particular company.

Acknowledgments

I HAD THE OPPORTUNITY to write this book during the beautiful, warm, sunny days sailing around the Åland islands, between Sweden and Finland. My deepest thanks to my husband, Olli Östring, who has given me the time to write this book while finding activities for our lovely children, Eric, age 6, and Veronica, age 12. Next year, I promise to play in the seaweed with you on the islands. Also my deepest thanks to my supportive mother, Kyllikki Lahdemaki, who has helped our family by taking care of our children on the many occasions when my husband and I needed to concentrate on our work.

I am very grateful to have had the opportunity to work with so many outstanding professionals and to get their feedback about this book and their guidance in concentrating on key points in supplier management. Timo Korvenpaa has given many valuable comments based on his expertise in finance and controlling. I am also grateful to my previous superior, David Hartley, for his comments on this book about the field of global business controlling. I am grateful to Mikko Routti and Petri Toivanen for their guidance and support in risk management.

I am grateful to Jorma Nyberg, who has provided support based on his knowledge about sourcing; to Adel Hattab, for his expertise and knowledge of collaboration and sourcing; to Pekka Lohiniva, for his comments based on his long experience in sourcing; and to Markku Jarventausta, for his valuable comments on sourcing. I am also grateful to Ruth Lyburn, for her creative and valuable comments from a research and development point of view; and to Mari Pekki, for her encouraging feedback. I owe thanks to Raija Ilvesmaki, Kathleen Kuosmanen, and Karen Scott.

I also had the pleasure of working for two years in Britain in the same office as the late Frank McGovern, an excellent mentor who encouraged me to start a corporate analysis of suppliers. I am very grateful for his mentoring and support.

I wish to express my deepest gratitude to those who helped make this publication a reality, especially Neil Levine, senior acquisitions editor at AMACOM Books, and Erika Spelman, associate editor.

Part One

A Strategy for Analyzing Your Suppliers

Why Analyze Your Suppliers?

1.1 A Changing Business Environment

The most significant drivers of a business are growth and profit for the owners. Nobody wants to make unprofitable investments. Owners calculate the relationship between risk and rewards. Choosing a supplier is a decision made exactly like any other risk decision in the company. However, the selection of suppliers is becoming an increasingly strategic decision. In the past, the selection of suppliers focused on the quality of the components. In today's business world, a supplier's internal processes, management of those processes, and business financing have increased in importance because the supplier is now sharing the business risk with the company it services.

The success of a company is a combination of decisions to be made and risks to be taken. By increasing flexibility, the management of a company expands its freedom of choice. A company increases its flexibility by optimizing the flexibility of its environment. As a company's dependency on suppliers increases, so does the importance of ensuring that those suppliers will meet the company's needs. Tight customer-supplier alliances have traditionally existed in some countries. In Japan, suppliers have been members of their customers' *keiretsu* (a group of interrelated companies around a major bank or industrial enterprise) for delivering to only one customer. A supplier is flexible for its sole customer's needs.

The typical features of moving from a traditional supplier relationship to a new approach with suppliers have caused several changes in the nature of the relationship between companies: for example, an increase in commitments. In order to maintain flexibility, a company must ensure the flexibility of its supplier chain in the new methods. By analyzing suppliers, the company has a tool for increasing flexibility by having a better overall understanding of its supplier. Because supplier analyses support the selection of good suppliers, they have a positive impact on profitability.

Wide Range vs. Focused

In the classic approach, a company produced everything internally. One example is the Ford Motor Company in the 1920s. A wide-range enterprise was the predominant feature in the classic approach; but in the new approach, there is a new driver of business: a focused enterprise. A focused enterprise concentrates on those tasks the outcome of which directly affects the competitive advantage of the company in its targeted markets and adds to the company's stock value. The area of focus depends on which business the company wants to be involved in.

A wide-range enterprise was involved in several business areas. All the areas had an impact on the business, but none had a significant impact exceeding other areas. (See Figure 1-1.) Housekeeping

Figure 1-1. The classic approach in a traditional environment—a company and its relationship to its suppliers.

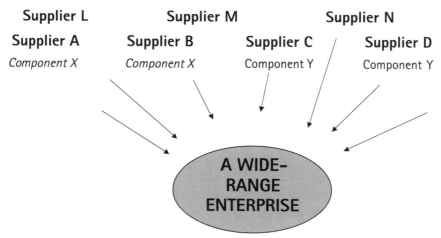

and travel arrangements are typical tasks that might not be the focus areas of a manufacturing company. There is no need for a unique way to execute those tasks other than an efficient and standardized manner to save time and resources. Each company has its own strategy and approach to business. A company may choose the traditional approach of being a wide-range enterprise, the new approach of being a focused enterprise, or a combination of the two. If your company wants to be a focused enterprise, you should find a reliable supplier to outsource the nonfocus tasks. A task can still be critical to company performance even when it does not belong to your focus business area. If your supplier fails, it will affect you!

A. The Classic Approach

Traditionally, companies were vertically integrated internally. A company's key to success was to own the largest resource base, manufacturing plants, and research laboratories, as well as the best distribution channels to support its production lines. Companies focused on producing components; therefore, the quality of these components was essential. In supplier evaluation, an essential aspect was quality control.

Every company was a wide-range enterprise by managing the entire business environment—from cleaning its premises to transporting products with its own vehicles to customers. The total supply chain was in the hands of the company. All employees were on the company's payroll: cleaning staff, drivers for company cars, engineers, factory workers, and information technology (IT) personnel. The company mostly owned production machinery, vans, trucks, and even vessels to transport goods. Moreover, the company internally produced most or all the components for its products.

If the company did not produce a particular component, there were several suppliers available for obtaining that component. The tenure of contract was normally short. Therefore, it was easy to substitute one supplier with another. Price and quality were some of the driving forces for choosing a supplier. A mass market of standardized products existed in the traditional environment. The repeated marketing messages were promoted to achieve volume goals.

The Classic Approach

❑ Internal production
❑ Mainly component suppliers

❑ Several suppliers of the same component in the market
❑ Easier to substitute one supplier with another
❑ Longer product life cycle—market changed slowly
❑ Few product models

B. The New Approach

The style of managing the supplier relationship has changed. Superior products do not necessarily provide the only sustainable competitive edge. In the new approach, it is easy to clone or reproduce products. The advantages of mass production are available to every company through purchased production capacity.

There are several differences among suppliers when comparing the new approach with the classic approach. Some of the most notable changes are the longer tenure of contracts and the lower number of suppliers. Suppliers are creating networks made up of fewer suppliers delivering complete products to a company. In tiered arrangements, the first-tier supplier has a direct relationship with the customer. The suppliers in the second, third, or lower tiers deliver to the first-tier supplier. Each supplier is more significant to a company than was the case previously. A smaller number of suppliers is making more complicated parts or entire products for your company. The first-tier suppliers are dependent on the second-tier and lower-tier suppliers. The entire supplier chain must be flexible to enable the focused enterprise to succeed. In Figure 1-2, supplier B is the first-

Figure 1-2. The new approach—a company and its relationship to its suppliers.

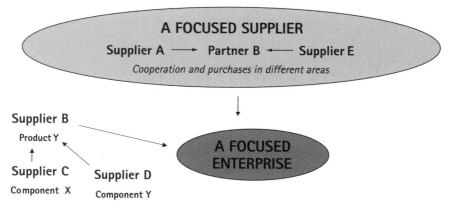

tier supplier and suppliers C and D are second-tier suppliers. The essential part in supplier evaluation is not simply quality; you should evaluate your supplier's processes and skills as a partner. Your supplier is an integrated part of your business risk. An increasing number of suppliers are more like partners, not merely suppliers for certain components.

As a result of the new approach, the supplier chain is longer than before. It is no longer simply your component supplier and your company. Instead, your supplier has several subsuppliers, who also have subsuppliers themselves. Orchestrating the entire supplier chain takes a greater effort than before.

The New Approach

- ❏ There are fewer suppliers.
- ❏ Each supplier is more important.
- ❏ There are more complex products.
- ❏ The supplier chain is longer—more players are in the supplier chain.
- ❏ The supplier's ability to change with its customer is increasingly important.
- ❏ Relationships are strategic.

Outsourcing

Outsourcing is the strategy of using external companies to provide a service or to manufacture products for your company. Outsourcing increases flexibility. Which products and services should you buy from outside companies? Which should you make internally? The tasks that are not made internally are outsourced.

The strategy that is chosen becomes a guideline for outsourcing: Does your company want to be a focused company? What is your focus area now and possibly in the future? Your focus area is the area of business in which you add the most value to customers. You should not outsource your current or future focus area; otherwise, you create a significant risk to your business. Your outsourcer—the company that is currently extending your flexibility—may evolve into your future competitor. There is a risk involved in outsourcing your focus business or parts of your focus business.

However, outsourcing increases when the market changes to a mass market, such as the markets for personal computers. In a mass market, *standardization* increases—outsourcers are seeking standardization. When your company is a focused enterprise, your business seeks differentiation. Among the services typically outsourced are housekeeping, transport management, medical, training, catering, and office supplies—but only if these are not focus areas of your company. A company might also outsource logistic chain management, research and development (R&D), and production. It is not only a question of outsourcing something; in many cases, it is a question of having deep cooperation between companies. It could even be said that the companies are alliances.

However, it must be remembered that outsourcing is not always a choice. Some companies have turned to outsourcing in response to corporate downsizing. By outsourcing, a company reduces the head count and assets. A lighter organization is expected to boost profit.

1.2 Supplier Base Management—Daily Activities

Each supplier adds value for a customer—the more value-adding suppliers you have, the more satisfied customers you are likely to have. The added value comes from innovative and efficient suppliers. Outsourcing decreases the number of suppliers. There are fewer suppliers to analyze. However, you should ensure that your first-tier supplier is analyzing its own suppliers' performance. The decision to analyze suppliers must be made on a case-by-case basis. First, the significance of analyzing the supplier is discussed, and then the analysis of the entire supplier base takes place.

The first step is to analyze your supplier. A more comprehensive analysis, here called a *corporate analysis,* is needed to analyze your supplier's performance if the following conditions exist:

❑ You don't have any previous experience with the supplier, so you need to assess a new supplier.

❑ You need to evaluate and follow up a performance of an existing supplier.

❑ You are having problems with an existing supplier.

❑ You are seeing warning flags.

The second step is to extend the analysis to the supplier base. All suppliers together form the supplier base. A suitable supplier base increases the efficiency of your company and your own profit.

The supplier base analysis is used in the following situations:
- ❏ To compare suppliers
- ❏ To optimize the number of suppliers
- ❏ To find stronger suppliers

Supplier Level

This section addresses asssessing new suppliers, evaluating and tracking the performance of a supplier, and problems and warning flags with existing suppliers.

Assessing a New Supplier

A new supplier is needed when current suppliers lack flexibility, capacity, or suitable products or when additional stimulation to the current supplier base is needed. A new supplier must be analyzed when no previous purchasing history is available. You should at least have an idea about the kind of company you are dealing with.

In a long-term relationship, both parties need to make significant investments, so an in-depth analysis of the supplier is important at the beginning of the relationship. If you have promised something over the longer term, you should be certain that you will be able to make it work. The effort to build the relationship covers all areas: strategic, technical, quality, financial, information flows, logistics, and possibly marketing. Changing suppliers is easy when you have only a short-term relationship.

Evaluating and Tracking the Supplier's Performance

Evaluating and tracking a supplier's performance is a continuous process. If the supplier demonstrates excellent performance at the peak of up markets, it may not necessarily keep its position during down markets. A company may lose creativeness and an ability to launch innovative products if talented personnel are leaving the company. Changes in the business environment make it essential to conduct an analysis periodically to monitor and develop the mutual relationship.

Problems with an Existing Supplier

The difficulties in dealing with a supplier may be as simple as the poor financial performance of the supplier. A poor financial position normally has a negative effect on quality and growth and may cause delivery problems. Dissatisfied subsuppliers might even turn to your company to demand payment. Unpaid bills can delay deliveries to your supplier and cause higher prices. All these factors can reflect in your supplier's deliveries to you. It is critical to uncover the real reason behind late deliveries.

Warning Flags

It is difficult to point out problems when times are good. Even when a problem is pointed out, the warning might not receive the attention it deserves. By identifying signs of trouble before they grow, you, as a customer, can take corrective steps on a proactive, rather than reactive, basis.

The key factor with warning flags is unexpected and sudden changes. One sign alone doesn't mean a crisis for a company. Several signs at the same time create uncertainty. The supplier's performance should be analyzed, because the risk in dealing with the supplier is increasing. It is recommended that a company examine warning flags in the following areas:

- ❑ Environment (see Figure 1-3)
- ❑ Company (see Figure 1-4)
- ❑ Financial figures (see Figure 1-5)
- ❑ Other (see Figure 1-6)

Supplier Base Level

The starting point of a comprehensive analysis is the current performance of a supplier. After you have analyzed the performance of several suppliers, you can compare the suppliers.

Comparing Suppliers

If you want to find the best companies to be your suppliers, you should compare different aspects of the companies, such as quality, technology, reliability, trade record, and terms of contracts. A comprehensive and similar analysis of each supplier is essential for comparing suppliers. A comparison of suppliers is necessary especially if you are going to optimize the number of suppliers. You must find the best, strongest, and most suitable suppliers for your company.

Figure 1-3. Warning flags—environment.

Environment	Warning flags
• Political, economic	• Drastic political, regulatory, or economic changes in supplier's country
• Market	• Radical change in market
• Customer	• Loss of company's main customer
• Suppliers	• Unexpected difficulties with supplier's quality and deliveries
• Competition	• Severe competition

Figure 1-4. Warning flags—company.

Company	Warning flags
• Size of the company	• Quick change in number of personnel
• Core business	• Unexpected change in core business
• Management and other key personnel	• Several key people resign within a short period of time
• Lack of managerial depth	• A dominating person, a board with little input into decisions, or too large an administration team
• Ownership	• Significant change in ownership
• Company structure	• An unnecessarily complicated company structure
• Acquisitions, mergers	• Several acquisitions or mergers in a short period of time
• Technology	• Outdated technology, low R&D investments

Figure 1-5. Warning flags—financial figures.

Financial figures	Warning flags
• Reliability and accuracy in current financial information	• Business decisions may be based on wrong assumptions
• Financial information	• Delay in providing financial information is a symptom of financial difficulties
• Changes in accounting policies	• In some cases, there are good reasons to change accounting policies, but changing it often indicates financial "game"
• Significant operational losses	• Losses increase suddenly and are substantial compared to the size of the business
• Equity	• The risk of bankruptcy increases and future funding is in danger if equity is decreasing significantly
• Current ratio	• The risk of liquidity problem increases if current liabilities exceed current assets
• Assets	• There is significant selling of assets

Figure 1-6. Warning flags—other.

Other	Warning flags
• Payment terms	• A supplier suddenly requires significantly shorter payment terms
• Share value	• There is a quick drop in share value and existing or starting financial difficulties
• Significant asset selling	• A supplier tries to increase cash and pay debts
• Strong downward trend in credit rating	• Interest margins increase when credit rating is dropping
• Significant restructuring and organizational changes	• A supplier downsizes its business, possibly affecting deliveries to your company

Optimizing the Number of Suppliers

Your company may have 500 suppliers, partners, and subcontractors, or perhaps the number is higher than 1,000. You need to optimize the number of suppliers. It would be cost-effective, easier, and more efficient for you to manage them. This creates economies of scale, while giving all remaining suppliers a larger business. It is a win-win situation. Before you close a working relationship, you need to evaluate your suppliers. That is when you must consider which suppliers are important to you and why.

Finding Stronger Suppliers

One reason to use suppliers rather than producing in-house is to increase cost efficiency, competence, and flexibility. The change from a classic to new approach of supplier relationship—the trend toward deeper cooperation and outsourcing—makes your suppliers even more valuable to you. If you choose a weak supplier, your customers might start seeing you as a weak supplier. Why? The quality of your products may decline and your deliveries may be inaccurate, for example. How do you add to the value of your products with poor suppliers?

Measurement Systems

During the first phase, you need to evaluate your suppliers and their compatibility with your strategies and needs. The evaluation is an ongoing process, although it is more vital at the beginning of the relationship. Later you know your suppliers better, so the reevaluation is easier.

During the second phase, you must have good measurement systems to verify and develop the value creation. Measuring offers the highest value for the customer and supplier because it is a mutual process. The results are evaluated together, and the action points are developed and agreed upon for mutual trust. Measurement and metrics (a set of impartial measures) in different areas are needed. Metrics are used as elements of rating systems to assess progress toward objectives, to set priorities, to spot issues, to indicate corrective actions, to allocate business among suppliers, to select new suppliers, and to further develop the supplier base.

Some metrics can be used for the company; other metrics can be used on a plant-by-plant basis, a commodity group basis, or a product basis.

The more often a company analyzes its suppliers, the earlier it can spot future possibilities and problem areas. However, frequent analysis and comprehensive measurement requires resources: It is time-consuming and costly, and it requires expertise.

Quality audits are not necessarily conducted on the top suppliers, but on those suppliers whose scores in some sector indicate lower-than-acceptable performance. The best-performing supplier can make a self-assessment in some areas. However, the company, as its customer, must carefully determine the areas in which self-assessment is valuable. The fact of the matter is that the supplier is selling to your company and is trying to keep its customer, especially if your company is one of its top customers.

Quality can be defined in quality audits. In addition to quality audits, separate security and environmental audits can be made. However, security and environmental audits are not discussed here in more detail. Auditing is an official examination of a defined matter or entity. Auditing is often connected to finances or quality. (Financial statement audits are discussed in Chapter 4.) Quality audits are an essential element in verifying the quality of the supplier, partner, or collaborator.

Customer satisfaction, customer requirements, and customer needs are the impetus of quality. Well-known quality system standards are ISO 9001 and ISO 9002.

A compliance audit asks, "Does this system, as implemented, meet the requirements laid down by a specific standard?" and, on the other hand, "Does the product or service audited comply with the specification and/or customer requirements?" Auditing determines whether the object of the audit is acceptable or unacceptable and specifies corrective actions.

Quality

Quality is an essential part of the supplier's performance. The classic approach pointed out the price and quality of products. The new approach extends the calculation from a single measurement to a comprehensive understanding of the supplier.

Quality was one of the most important areas in the classic approach to the supplier relationship. By no means has the significance of quality disappeared. A supplier with low quality causes difficulties. Quality is relatively easy to measure with specific metrics or more comprehensively by conducting quality audits, which can identify areas needing more attention. Quality audits cover areas such as management systems, manufacturing, engineering, administration, purchasing, environment, and risk management. Typically, quality audits consist of the following parts: acceptable or unacceptable; and needs improvement, that is, unacceptable and corrective actions. The meaning of quality here is understood as how the product meets the customer's needs.

The severity of issues occasionally encountered by all companies in different areas varies to some extent. Through effective metrics and communication, it is easier to follow the development in different areas. If a supplier rating drops below a certain level, the first action is a discussion with the supplier to identify problem areas and verify suggested solutions. If the problem is easy or possible to fix, the outcome will be positive and the corrective actions will solve the problem.

To what extent is it reasonable and feasible to go with the requirements of corrective actions? There comes a point where you must consider changing suppliers if improvements will take too long or if the supplier is too much of a risk and your deliveries to your customers are in danger.

The new approach with deeper cooperation with the supplier requires more attention to the supplier relationship than the classic approach with several suppliers. The importance of analyzing and measuring the supplier and the supplier base performance in quality and other business areas has increased.

Key Points

❑ *Take into account changes in the business environment.* Changes from the classic approach of business (in-house production) to the new approach (outsourcing) generally have increased the significance of suppliers. In outsourcing, the relationship is strategic and typically involves a long-term commitment, so it is not easy to change a supplier.

❑ *Find the relevance of evaluation and analysis.* The need to evaluate a supplier is most significant when the supplier is new or there are problems with the supplier. Evaluation of a supplier's performance is not a onetime action; it should be a continuous process. The key warning flags about a supplier require special attention, especially if several warning flags exist simultaneously. The focus should be on a limited number of deep and critical relationships, rather than on numerous unmonitored relationships.

❑ *Enlarge the analysis from a supplier to the overall supplier base to compare suppliers.* By comparing the suppliers in different areas, such as quality, and the supplier as a company, it is possible to find stronger suppliers. Comparison is also essential when optimizing the number of suppliers. The best suppliers increase your flexibility.

❑ *Measure the performance of the supplier.* Comparison is made easier by measuring suppliers. One of the most typical areas to measure is quality.

❑ *Continue auditing on a regular basis and involve benchmarking methodology.* By continuous quality and quantity audits, you will be able to effectively follow the quality of the supplier's products on a regular basis. By benchmarking suppliers, you can find the differences and areas to develop.

❑ *Read between the lines.* Your supplier might not immediately tell you the truth about its difficulties. You may need to find the untold story. Use analysis to create the picture of the supplier's financial and business strengths.

Case 1: Supplier in Trouble

"The listing of NewCCC Inc. on NASDAQ was halted. Your auditors wanted to see the conclusions of a forensic audit of NewCCC Inc.'s books going back to 1999. The forensic audit is looking for potential fraud," Jill Turner stated, looking at the pale fifty-year-old man sitting in front of her.

"The listing of our shares was halted temporarily," he pointed out, tapping his finger on the table as he spit out "temporarily."

"When will the listing continue?" Jill asked, trying to decipher the meaning of the word *temporarily.*

The meeting room was small—only four chairs and a table. James Mendelsson, senior vice president of NewCCC Inc., was sitting on the edge of his chair in front of

Jill. He reluctantly admitted that he didn't know of any schedule for the listing. "We expect that the forensic audit will be finished by the end of August," he explained. Jill, the business analyst for suppliers, wondered how many times he had told the same story. It was obvious that investors, bankers, shareholders, employees, suppliers, and customers wanted to know what had happened to this relatively old and stable company.

"There's still three months to go before your forensic audit will be finished," Jill said impatiently, and continued, "Your previous CFO and controller had to leave the company. Is that correct?"

James nodded tiredly and moved forward in his chair, his dark blue eyes locked on the simple brown table.

"Are there any pending lawsuits against NewCCC Inc.?" Jill asked.

"No, not at this moment," James sounded delighted to break the news. He held his head in his hands. "We are investigating what happened," he emphasized.

"Who is your biggest shareholder? Do you still have the same shareholders as before?" Jill asked and looked at James. He was quiet—no answer.

"It was announced in your annual report in March 2002 that the biggest share-holders were your president and chairman, John O'Malley, with 55 percent of shares, and your previous CFO, Timothy Credit, with 10 percent of shares. Is this information still valid?" Jill inquired.

"I can't say exactly who our biggest shareholders are at the moment. I suppose that it's still the same people as before," James said in a hesitating voice, staring at the table again.

"Please check out the details for me," Jill asked in a friendly but firm tone and continued, "Do you have that information available?"

"All right, Kate, please get the files from my office," James said, turning to the accountant who was sitting next to him. Kate left the room. To Jill, the seconds felt like hours as they waited for Kate's return. "More coffee?" James asked politely.

"Yes, please. With milk, but no sugar. Thanks."

Kate returned to the small meeting room carrying some papers. James nodded to Kate to sit. He took the papers and flicked through them until he found the relevant page. His expression changed. "Well, there have been some changes in our ownership, I see," he stated, looking as if he had seen the information for the first time.

This was not a surprise, Jill thought wryly to herself. She said to James, "According to the news, your president and CFO sold the largest portion of their shares just one month before this case started."

"Yes, you are right," confirmed James slowly. "Of course, our management expects everything to be all right in accounting," James pointed out strongly.

Jill had another opinion about the link between the occurrences. Top management must be aware of the possible "creative accounting" that helped the company to show higher profits. The chair and CFO made significant gains by selling their shares at a good price because other outside investors believed NewCCC Inc. to be in ex-cellent financial condition. The accounting might be misleading. The share price increased while top management possibly presented overly optimistic financial state-ments. Jill was quiet as she jotted down more notes.

This company was the main supplier for the new products in which Success Inc., Jill's employer, had already invested $50 million. Jill's colleagues had conducted a quality audit on this company. The result of the quality audit was good—only three nonconformities. Until now, nobody had made a comprehensive analysis of the financial status and management of the company, which could reveal the weak points of the supplier. Jill's colleagues launched a supplier analysis when NewCCC Inc. had to leave NASDAQ. It was obvious that the warning flags of the company's financial condition were in place.

Should Success Inc. seek another supplier? It would take at least two months to find a new supplier. The project would be delayed, and production would start much later than planned. Success Inc. would lose approximately $100 million. How much would the delay affect Success Inc.'s market share? The risk and the calculated potential loss were high. Jill sipped some cold coffee from her cup in the dark meeting room. Success Inc. needs to find a way to reduce the risk.

Choosing Which Suppliers to Analyze

2.1 Understanding Risk

This chapter discusses the general meaning of risk and risk management, as well as how the objectives and goals of risk management support the selection of suppliers that need to be analyzed and at what level. There are always two possible outcomes associated with risk—and at least one of them is undesirable. There is no risk if you know for certain that a loss will occur. Risk is associated with profit and the possibility of loss. The following example shows the effect that risk factors might have.

A supplier's poor financial condition is a risk factor that might cause a risk event, such as delays in payments to subsuppliers or even bankruptcy. To evaluate a risk outcome, you can estimate the possible effects on key objectives. For example, the risk outcome to your company might be a delay or interruption in deliveries to your own suppliers. When you find the possible risk outcome, you might try to eliminate or mitigate it—or even to accept it. Finding a replacement for a focused supplier could take time, thereby causing delays in your deliveries and, consequently, risking your reputation with your customers. The outcome of the realization of the risk factor is a loss in monetary terms, that is, a utility loss.

Understanding and dealing with business risks is essential for every company. In every company, the top management should approve the company's risk policy. The risk policy itself does not create significant added value to the company if it is not implemented at the operational level. The approved risk management approach should align with the company's objectives.

Objectives of Risk Management

The risk management vision must define the scope of taking risks. Risk taking should enable a company to achieve profitable growth. There should be an understanding of risks and an agreed-upon level of risk taking. The objectives of risk management include two components: understanding and control. Understanding includes components such as risk awareness and feasible control. Control means that every supplier relationship is prone to risks and that in some relationships risks occur. Risk management is an investment in the future. It is better to anticipate possible problems than to spend a significant amount of time solving problems. Risk management improves the predictability and control of projects. If you have a tight supplier relationship with a company that is financially weak, the probability of delivery delays is higher than with a financially sound supplier.

Goals and Stakeholders

Goals are generally practical, such as the delivery of specific products on schedule at expected costs. There are several stakeholders such as customers, purchasing managers, purchasing departments, and logistics departments. Evaluating risks and what needs to be done should be viewed objectively. However, it is important to find the main stakeholders and their interests. It is necessary to prioritize the objectives of the key stakeholders and to be aware of the overall objective. Purchasing managers are presumably the ones responsible for keeping deliveries on schedule in their own commodity area. The head of the purchasing or sourcing department is responsible for the overall sourcing function and its flexibility. The risk of delayed deliveries belongs to the sourcing department and a specific purchasing manager; therefore, the key person in the supplier risk is the purchasing manager.

2.2 Risk Categories

A company's general risk management principles should be based on identifying key risks, such as:

1. *Strategic risks.* Risks must be taken into account in strategies. There is a correlation among strategy planning, decision making, and risk analysis.

2. *Operational risks.* Sourcing belongs to operational risks. The quality, correct timing, and scheduling of materials; optimal pricing; and supply interruption can be categorized under sourcing risks. A poor supplier base is a potential factor in sourcing risks.

3. *Hazard risks.* Hazard risks cause damage to assets (for example, buildings or machinery) or intellectual assets (for example, brand or product liabilities). Typically, hazard risks can be insured.

4. *Financial risks.* Financial risk is the threat of losing an asset or income. Thus, financial risk involves two elements: (1) the individual or organization that is exposed to loss, and (2) the asset or income whose destruction or dispossession will cause financial loss. Financial risks are often related to the treasury function.

Credit Risk vs. Supplier Risk

Managing supplier risk is not the same as managing credit risk. Your company's financial department spends time checking out customers before granting them fifteen-day, thirty-day, or even sixty-day credit for purchases. What type of analysis does your company conduct of suppliers when considering a ten-year supply agreement with them? The same quick credit check is perhaps not adequate for a long-term supplier relationship. The tenure of contracts with your supplier is longer than in years past. The new approach in the customer-supplier relationship has changed. The new approach is to enter into strategic alliances and to turn to outsourcing and just-in-time inventory control, thus increasing the dependency on the suppliers' timing.

Cooperation with your outsourcer—that is, a company producing a product or service for you—is generally much deeper than cooperation with your traditional suppliers. The outsourcer is shouldering some of your business risks, but at the same time, you have a new risk to orchestrate with your counterpart. To reduce your counterpart's risk, you should improve your knowledge of your counterpart.

You must analyze the different aspects of your outsourcer—not only the aspects related to its product, quality, and availability but also the aspects related to credit perspective.

From a credit perspective, a poor supplier might have poor delivery accuracy because of its own financial difficulties in paying its suppliers. When selecting your strategic suppliers, you should spend time qualifying your suppliers from a credit perspective.

2.3 Risk Management

Risk management does not mean risk avoidance. Risk management activities should ensure that the shareholders' assets and revenue are protected. A tangible aspect in risk management is the implementation of safety measures in a factory or the establishment of a backup or contingency plan in case of loss of a major supplier or client. Risk management is a continuous process where the risks of operations and products are analyzed systematically. Purchasing managers can analyze and monitor the risks of their own commodity area by using the companywide accepted methods and tools.

Barry W. Boehm has established clear steps in software risk management. Similar steps can also be used in overall risk management to enable you to follow the path from the meaning of risk to finding the tools for identifying possible risks and managing them. In Boehm's model (see Figure 2-1), risk management can be divided into two main categories—risk assessment and risk control—which are used to find the respective steps in analyzing supplier risks.

Risk Assessment

Risk assessment includes risk identification: Supplier risks should be identified by checklists based on historic experience and by open brainstorming based on potential risks. First, the purpose of identifying risks is to find the potential threats to delivering your products. Second, you should identify which suppliers pose the biggest threat to your company's production.

A performance model of supplier risk can provide detailed descriptions of a supplier's risks so that the highest risk scenarios and appropriate risk control actions can be planned and implemented. Once the risks of the supplier are identified and analyzed, the next step is to prioritize, or rank, the risk items. If resources for analyses are limited, it may not be feasible to analyze all suppliers. Instead,

Figure 2-1. Risk management steps.

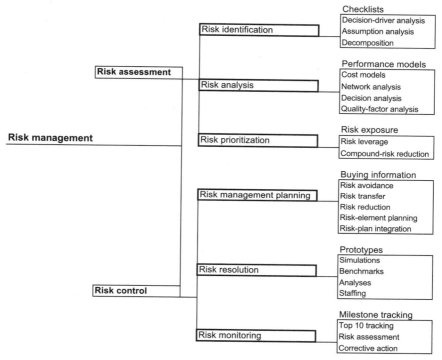

Source: B. W. Boehm, "Software Risk Management: Principles and Practices," *IEEE Software*, vol. 8, no. 1 (1991): 32–33 © 1991 IEEE. Reprinted with permission.

you should focus more time and resources on analyzing the most important suppliers. In order to do this, it is necessary to rank the suppliers.

Risk Control

Risk control is divided into the following elements:

❑ Risk management planning prepares you to address each risk item. Planning helps you to achieve the goal of managing supplier risks.

❑ Risk resolution produces a situation in which the risk items are managed as planned or otherwise resolved.

❑ Risk monitoring helps to continuously monitor the status of your supplier risk. To monitor your supplier risk, you can implement practical risk assessment.

Methods and Tools

Risk management methods and tools can help achieve goals. Simple methods should be used at the beginning. Common sense is one of the best methods; later, you can develop or buy methods that are more complex. The purpose of using a supplier evaluation tool is to create a systematic approach for evaluating supplier risks in a company. The tool can produce a scorecard that categorizes risks into high, medium, and low risks. The monetary value of the risk should be evaluated.

2.4 Classify Your Suppliers and Create a Strategy for Analysis

After learning more about risks and risk management, the type of analysis needed to analyze suppliers will be defined. One way to choose the type of analysis is to define the possible risk of losses, which can be calculated by using risk management tools and methods.

You have several choices when introducing the analysis techniques into your organization:

❑ You can teach all purchasing managers to do a quick analysis (financial analysis) themselves.

❑ You can provide a corporate analysis from an internal or external specialist.

❑ You can combine the previous two systems (see Chapter 3).

Choose the Type of Analysis

The optimal way to increase your knowledge about your supplier is to find the best way to analyze suppliers. The method and type of analysis must be defined based on the degree of risk for losses—in other words, how much your company will potentially lose if this supplier fails.

Time is money. On one hand, it is a waste of money to make a comprehensive analysis of a standard commodity supplier that is readily replaceable with other suppliers. On the other hand, it is a critical mistake to ignore a risk and drop a critical supplier without having conducted any analysis. The impact on your business can be substantial.

The supplier risk can be understood and calculated in several ways, such as:

❑ Loss in monetary value

❑ Estimated loss in the event of nondelivery or delayed delivery

❑ Anticipated loss of reputation

❑ Possible loss of customers and market share

Supplier risk is the driving force behind specifying the type of analysis that is made of the suppliers. If the potential loss is high, the supplier analysis should be more comprehensive, such as a corporate analysis. A short analysis or check is recommended for companies with a lower risk. (See Table 2-1.)

Table 2-1. Risk level and analysis.

Risk level	Nature of relationship	Type of analysis
Low	Easy to change a supplier	No analysis, just a short credit report
Middle	Relatively easy to change	Short analysis
High	Difficult to change a supplier	Corporate analysis

In the new approach, the supplier relationship in terms of wide range or focused can also serve the idea of how to classify your suppliers for different types of analysis. You determine your focus area and classify your suppliers based on their focus areas. Focus suppliers can be those suppliers that are most essential to your business—you can't afford to miss opportunities and those suppliers. Your nonfocus suppliers can be suppliers that pose less risk for your business, such as cleaning providers or office stationary suppliers. The risk to your company is generally low if you lose an indirect, nonfocus supplier.

The supplier risk can be partly defined through supplier segments, dividing suppliers into different risk categories based on the following: the possibilities and the highest estimated loss to change the supplier. If your company is too dependent on any one company, finding another source of supply can be difficult.

The following definitions of a supplier can be used: sole source, single source, and multiple sources. There are limits by optimizing the number of suppliers: All suppliers do not have the same technology. Therefore, backup sources are needed in the event of quality, quantity, or other problems (see Table 2-2).

Table 2-2. Sources.

Source	Number of sources	Number of locations
Sole	One	One
Single	One	Several
Multiple	Two or more	More locations

Sole Source

There is only one company with one location. It is difficult to substitute a sole source. The risk is relatively high with a sole source because of the high dependency on the company. Is the company the sole source of a special part? Is the company a sole source for a standard item?

Single Source

The risk is slightly lower with a single source than it is with a sole source. A single source has one supplier with several locations. The dependency on a company exists, but the multiple locations reduce the location-specific risks, such as the possibility of a natural disaster, national regulations, or local instability. Which type of products or services is the company delivering: special or standard?

Multiple Sources

The supplier risk is lower when there are two or more suppliers with several locations. The combination carrying the highest risk for a company is the sole source supplier—one source and one location—with a potentially high risk for monetary loss. A sole source supplier of a special component presents a high-risk situation.

A single source supplier with multiple locations falls within the high-risk category if the potential monetary risk is high. Even if the supplier has several locations, it is still a matter of being the same company. The company might be in a financial downturn that could affect all its locations. The parent company controls the investment and financial flows of the company group. In the new approach, several significant suppliers, outsourcers, and collaborators belong to the high-risk category.

In the case of a multiple source supplier in the high-risk category, there are two or more suppliers and potential suppliers to take orders that cannot be placed with the original supplier. However, the other suppliers may lack the capacity that is needed at that specific time. In the case of significant high-risk suppliers, a comprehensive corporate analysis should be made of all suppliers.

Key Suppliers with High Volume

The most important suppliers are the key suppliers—that is, focus suppliers with high volume. If you expect a small supplier to deliver high volumes, your assumption may not be correct. The key supplier with high volume is likely to be a large company. In some cases, however, a small company might be able to produce high volumes.

A Large Company as a Supplier

Do you know what share your purchases account for out of the supplier's total revenue? If you are a minority customer, you normally do not have to worry about investments the supplier might need to make to increase its capacity.

A large company usually has better financial strength to carry its investments than a small company. However, a large company can face difficulties in the market and thereby cut its costs. It is possible that the division you are interested in does not even belong to the focus business of the company. Try to determine whether you are dealing with the supplier's focus business. Is the company going to expand the division or subsidiary that you are dealing with? Is the company going to divest the division or subsidiary? If so, who would be a potential buyer? The supplier may ask your opinion of the merger or acquisition if you are a top customer. The acquisition or merger might also come as a surprise to you. Are you prepared for changes? Do you have a backup plan in the event that your significant supplier is sold to your competitor? What is your importance to the supplier?

A Small Company as a Supplier

If your company's purchases account for a major share of your supplier's revenue, you have the advantage of being a key customer whose needs the supplier is trying to fulfill. You are dealing with its focus business. If you fail, your supplier fails. The relationship is mutual.

However, your small supplier may not have the financial strength to make necessary investments. The supplier's banker may recommend that they turn to your company to negotiate financing, especially if you represent a solid, creditworthy company. Are you so dependent on this supplier's products that you are willing to provide it with financial support? It is vital to start an analysis of your key suppliers with a high volume, because they are your most important group of suppliers.

You must choose the appropriate type of analysis for evaluating your supplier base. In the case of a sole source supplier, it is normally a question of a small- or medium-size company, because the risk of having a sole source supplier is generally very high because of the limited financial and human resources that small- and medium-size companies usually have. However, you should not abandon all potentially high-risk small- and medium-size companies when refusing to operate with them, because you risk losing future challenging products in your product portfolio. The business risk is welcome when you know the level of your risk and you have a contingency plan. A wise manager takes calculated business risks.

Key Points

- ❏ Risk is the key driver to classify the analysis need.
- ❏ Risk management enables business to be continued in an optimal way in every circumstance. By analyzing your suppliers, you reduce the risk in sourcing, procurement, and R&D.
- ❏ By defining the degree of risk, you can determine the type of analysis that is needed. There is no need to analyze all suppliers in a similar way and some suppliers not at all. There is a need to concentrate on analyzing key suppliers with volumes.
- ❏ Define the different types of analysis needed for the supplier groups and suppliers. You will save time and money by choosing the right type of analysis. Make certain that at least the most important suppliers are analyzed.
- ❏ Determine how much of your business is the supplier's focus business in volumes compared to the supplier's size.

Case 2: Small Supplier, Big Volume

Part 1

As Jill sat in her office one late Thursday evening, she looked around and noticed a row of empty desks. Everyone had taken his or her laptop home. Outside, she saw the light on the street and the darkness of the sea. Outside, the world was gray and blurred.

She took a deep breath and folded her hands. She wondered what Success Inc. really knew about its suppliers. As a business analyst of suppliers, Jill Turner should know a lot about them. But what about the others in the company?

❑ The president of Jill's company, Success Inc., had a good personal relationship with some suppliers.

❑ The vice president of sourcing had also created upper-level connections with suppliers.

❑ The quality managers knew the exact quality of the components from different companies.

❑ Purchasing managers knew the whole relationship with the supplier and the contracts. Purchasing managers also had a good view of the products in their area.

❑ The risk manager was establishing overall risk knowledge and the ability to find and manage risks in the organization.

Jill's cell phone was ringing, even though it was already late—7 P.M.

"Jill Turner."

"Hi, Jill, it's Jack Smith from sourcing. I decided to give you a call because we've been e-mailing so much."

"I was thinking of doing the same, Jack," Jill replied. "As you saw in my report, I think that if we want ABC GmbH to put out those volumes, we have to be prepared to finance the investment."

"I don't know what made us think that ABC GmbH could do the investment on its own," Jack said, in a desperate voice, and continued, "We should have checked the financial position of ABC much earlier."

"Jack, ABC is a company that was involved in a management buyout just three months ago without any venture capitalists; in other words, financing has to be very tight in this company. ABC has to count every cent to be able to produce its main products. It won't be long before our product no longer belongs within the focus of its business. Has anyone even thought about this?" Jill asked, turning her chair toward her e-mail box, where she had just received a message from John Lyburn, vice president of sourcing.

She read the message and turned her concentration back to the conversation with Jack.

"Jack, did you have any suppliers other than ABC? Is there any chance of replacing the component with some other material?"

"I don't know. I'll have to discuss it with the R&D team. We should have made the decision to choose another supplier a long time ago. Elite Ltd would have been in great financial condition."

"Why didn't you choose Elite?" Jill asked curiously, turning back to check her e-mail, which read: "Team meeting tomorrow."

"I don't like the attitude of the guys at Elite. Tim really irritated me last time. He isn't very accommodating to our wishes."

"Maybe you should let their managing director know about it."

"I actually did, today," said Jack, laughing. "They asked me why we are not purchasing more. So, I told them to give me guys who are more cooperative. I don't like to be undervalued all the time."

Jill's voice was eager, "What was the conclusion?"

"Elite's managing director was quiet," Jack laughed.

"All right, Jack. Is it possible to change the supplier? If we don't, we'll end up with real problems," Jill said.

"I feel that ABC has planned on getting a really good profit to serve us and on getting us to pay for its other investments too," Jack said slowly.

"My sentiments exactly, Jack, but I didn't want to put it like that," Jill replied, leaning back in her chair. "You are definitely right, Jack. Please give more thought to the deal. If you want me to do something, give me a call."

"All right, Jill, I'll get back to you when I know something new."

Part 2

It was 9 A.M. Jill was standing with Purchasing Manager Jack Smith in the Berlin airport. They were waiting for Jurgen Wagner, account manager of ABC GmbH, who had arranged to meet them in the arrivals hall.

"Hello, Jurgen," Jack shouted and waved his hand.

Jurgen had short black hair. He was in his forties. He looked delighted to see Jack.

"Hello, Jack. Nice to see you here, again. It's been two weeks since we last met. Did you get the technical details I sent to you yesterday? Do you have an answer to the question?" Jurgen smiled. He didn't wait for an answer, but he wanted to show his interest toward the customer.

Still smiling, Jurgen turned toward Jill. "Jurgen Wagner," he warmly shook her hand. "Is this your first time in Berlin?" Jurgen turned around. He didn't expect an answer to his question as he offered to help carry Jill's briefcase.

"Jill Turner. Nice to see you. Yes, this is my first time in Berlin. Thank you, I can carry my briefcase myself."

"Oh, no, please, allow me," Jurgen said, and continued, "When are you flying back to Finland?"

"This evening at 6 o'clock."

"That's really a pity. Next time you'll have to stay longer to see more of Berlin."

They were outside. There was a little bit of snow here and there. Jill was curious, trying to guess which car was Jurgen's—the crimson Mercedes or the silver BMW? It was neither: Jurgen packed Jill's black briefcase into a small, dark, older model Opel.

After an hour, they arrived at the factory. Jurgen parked his car as close to the front door of the old factory building as possible. She quickly glanced around at the other cars. Some were rusty and older models, some were new—there was one glittering BMW. Jill was used to looking at the cars outside the factory. When she worked in banking, the question was, "Did the owner spend most of the borrowed capital to drive a nice car rather than develop the company?" Cars can say a great deal about the people and the company.

Jurgen opened the heavy door and they all walked up the wide steps to the upper floor.

They arrived in the vast meeting room. The furniture was mahogany, big and solid, and the chairs were covered with dark brown leather. Jill took off her coat, handed it to Jurgen, and sat down in a comfortable chair. Jack sat next to her. He opened his laptop and turned it to Jill. Speaking quietly, he asked: "Did you get this calculation? I ran some numbers myself and the investment plan looks like this. The needed financing for the investment is at least $20 million."

"That is a higher amount than mentioned before," Jill observed grimly and studied Jack's calculation. "Let's go through all the details of the investment," Jill whispered quickly.

At the same moment, Hans Huppert, the main owner and managing director, walked into the room with two other men. The newcomers shook hands with Jill and Jack and exchanged business cards.

The amount needed for the investment was presented as only $10 million. The supplier showed a lower amount of investment because it would be easier to get the customer involved in the investment. Later, it is easier to regret calculations that are too low when the customer has no way of turning back on the deal.

"Jack, is everything okay?" asked managing director Huppert, as he turned nervously and smiled at Jack.

"Unfortunately, I have to say that you are late with your schedule. Can you please explain," Jack said impatiently.

Jill studied the calculations.

Huppert turned to Jurgen and asked, "Is everything fine?" Jurgen started to quickly explain the problems, which Huppert already knew about without any explanations. Huppert nodded from time to time to show that he was following Jurgen's speech. Jill noted the hesitation, hardly perceptible, but nevertheless there, before Huppert bowed his head. "Yes, that is right . . ."

Jack interrupted, "Please, can we go directly to the matter? We need the line. You should have ordered the production line already."

There was silence.

Jill broke the silence by looking at the chief financial officer (CFO), an older man who had been quiet the entire time. "I suggest that we go through the main proposal first and then go into the details of the investment. According to this calculation, there are no financial gaps. Have you taken everything into account in the investment?"

"Everything we know at this point is there," Jurgen stated quickly.

The CFO, Frank Huismann, was still quiet.

"Jack, what is the time schedule? Is everything included here? What do you think?" Jill insisted, turning to Jack.

Jack had a clear opinion: "This schedule is incorrect. We should order the first production line now and the second line after a month. How many test drives are you going to run? Do you have raw material for the test runs?"

The supplier was playing a game, trying to trick Success Inc. with its calculations.

"I don't think that we should invest so quickly," started Jurgen, but Huismann interrupted him by holding up his right hand. Determined, he walked to the front of the room and started drawing a time schedule.

"You are right, we need to invest earlier and we need more financing. These calculations do not take into account the working capital that we need to run the pilot line. Working capital was not included in the calculations." Huismann looked at them with his dark eyes. He raised the paper in his hand and waved it. "This calculation was made for internal purposes. We included working capital in the other calculations. We recalculated the price of the lines based on the newest offers." Jill and Jack listened to him carefully. Huismann said when he had finished: "It is amazing, that—yes, it is amazing . . ."

Ultimately, their CFO agreed that the calculation didn't take into account all costs.

Jack sighed deeply. "What are the correct calculations?" he asked in a tired voice. "Last time, you said you needed $10 million in financing and now you are telling us something else. What is the correct figure? We need to know if we want to finance that investment or if we are going to back out of the investment," Jack continued.

There was a faint expression of delight on Jurgen's face. "You need the components for your new product X, which, you pointed out, would be your main product in the future," he reminded Jack and Jill. They were well aware of that fact. The R&D department of Success Inc. had decided to go with ABC GmbH's component. Nobody had thought that the company had to invest to produce huge volumes of components X and Y. Jack and Jill were here to find out the real financing needs.

"All right, let's start at the beginning," Jill said, now aware that this meeting would be much more difficult than she had anticipated.

The R&D team at Success Inc. had chosen the component produced by ABC GmbH. This often happens in real life. An R&D team finds a nice, innovative component but neglects to check whether or not the supplier can actually produce the required volumes. This is the dilemma between R&D and sourcing. R&D transfers demanding suppliers to sourcing for handling. If the supplier is a sole source, sourcing hardly has a chance of changing suppliers.

After three hours, a surprised Jill and Jack determined that the financing gap would amount to $50 million.

"Your taxi is here," Huppert announced. The entire management team escorted Jill and Jack downstairs.

"We really hope that we can make the investments as soon as possible," says Huppert, studying Jack's face. "If you have any questions about the calculations, please contact me," he adds.

"I imagine that we will have some additional questions," Jill replies as she gets into the taxi.

———

This small start-up company could not fulfill the supplier's requirements set in the supplier assessment process. The risk was taken to be successful in leading-edge products, but the risk was not properly assessed early enough in the R&D milestones of Success Inc. Jill and Jack found another supplier after a year. However, Success Inc. lost a lot of time and money with ABC GmbH. If Success Inc. had checked out the financial situation of its supplier before specifying ABC's components for the future product, it would have achieved significant savings.

Part Two

Components of a Corporate Analysis of Suppliers

3

Creating a Corporate Analysis

CORPORATE ANALYSIS INCLUDES all relevant information needed to analyze your supplier's financial and operational status. If your company has a limited number of small suppliers, purchasing managers can easily handle the investigation process informally or simply evaluate certain information. But when your company is dealing closely with a large number of suppliers that are substantially important for your products, some streamlining is essential. The corporate analysis format provides a systematic way to gather and evaluate information.

Credit-rating agencies, banks, financial communities, and research houses can provide an analysis. If you don't like to rely on the judgment of other people, you can conduct your own analysis, for example:

❑ *Conduct the analysis yourself or internally within the organization.* The analysis can be comprehensive or brief.

❑ *Build a consistent system for analyzing your suppliers.* If you ask a third party to build the system, you must at least know what you require from the system.

Corporate analysis includes a detailed analysis of the company's financial status and business prospects. However, it is too expensive to conduct a comprehensive analysis for all suppliers. Therefore, a shorter version—called a financial analysis (quick analysis)—is presented in Subchapter 6.1 in connection with the template tool. Financial analysis focuses on the company's financial statements and key ratios.

Corporate analysis consists of quantitative and qualitative analysis of the company. A corporate analysis is a comprehensive evaluation of your supplier's financial strength and operational performance and a forecast of future performance. The qualitative parts of the corporate analysis support the supplier's financial profile. They connect the analysis of financial figures with operational items. The structure of corporate analysis is presented in Figure 3-1.

In this book, the type of analysis that is referred to as *corporate analysis* includes the following components: an executive summary

Figure 3-1. Corporate analysis.

A   **EXECUTIVE SUMMARY**

Recommendations
Strengths, Weaknesses, Opportunities, and Threats (SWOT)
Conclusions
Risk rating

B   **ENVIRONMENT**
Country
Political environment
Regulatory environment

Market
Customers
Suppliers and logistics
Competitors

C   **COMPANY**
Strategy
Company life cycle
Technology
Ownership
Corporate structure
　　—Holding company
　　—Subsidiary
Organization
Management
Acquisitions and mergers

D   **FINANCIAL ANALYSIS**
Financial statements
Key ratios
Forecast

(including the recommendations and conclusions of the other parts such as environment, company, and financial analysis) and a risk rating (based on the financial position and other information about the company). The environment and company components represent the qualitative part of corporate analysis, while the financial analysis and forecast provide the quantitative analysis.

3.1 Quantitative Analysis

Quantitative analysis comprises the financial aspects. It is based on financial statements and ratios calculated from financial statements. The most important sources of information for evaluating the financial health of your supplier are financial statements, which include the balance sheet, statements of income, cash flow statement, and notes. The balance sheet shows the situation on a specific date in the past; the statement of income—also referred to as a profit and loss statement—shows the entity's financial performance during a specific period; the cash flow statement shows the source and use of funds; and the notes provide detailed information about the contents of the financial statements.

Financial strength can be found by analyzing financial statements. The analysis, which presents a company's historic (three to five years) financial performance and an assessment of the financial strength of the company, is presented in Chapter 4. It is important to learn to read financial statements, which usually conceal more than they reveal. You can learn more about your supplier's business through financial statements than you ever imagined.

The most suitable ratios are dependent on the purpose of the analysis. Slightly different ratios are used in the credit analysis of customers and investment analysis for equity investors than for supplier analysis. Table 3-1 presents financial ratios. You can choose all the ratios or focus on specific ratios when drawing out the core information.

Table 3-1. Financial ratios.

Ratios	
Growth	Revenue growth
Profitability	Operating margin, ROA (return on assets)
Liquidity	Current ratio, quick ratio
Leverage	Equity to total assets, interest coverage
Efficiency	Receivables, payables, and inventory turnover

Financial profiles do not necessarily hold good for any length of time in today's rapidly changing business environment. An acquisition can quickly alter a company's financial profile. After making a large acquisition, a previously profitable and stable company can become a loss-making business. Have you ever had a supplier that experienced difficulties after an acquisition?

Financial Analysis

Financial statements, which comprise the balance sheet, statements of income, and the cash flow statement, show the historical status of the company at the time defined in the financial statements. The verbal analysis and key ratios help the corporate analysis reader to evaluate the financial performance of the company.

The meaning of the figures and the conclusion about them indicate your supplier's short-term liquidity and its ability to repay debt. It also helps in categorizing companies and creates a more reliable risk rating for them. Companies in different industries operate within different ratios at any given rating when compared with another industry. Each industry has unique features and each company has different strengths and weaknesses within that industry.

Forecast

Several factors can affect a company's future. Internal factors such as strategy, technology, or product mix can be managed by the company itself. However, several external factors can influence the company's markets and environment. These factors are beyond the company's scope of influence. Forecasting is discussed in more detail in Subchapter 4.6.

3.2 Qualitative Analysis

Remember that financial reports are always historical data about the performance of the company. If the business environment is lucrative and the operations of the company are in good order, the financial result of the company will be good. If you do things right, the numbers will follow and vice versa. Therefore, it is necessary not only to study the financial figures but also to look at the various operational and environmental issues. Only then are you able to have a clear picture of the current performance of your supplier.

Qualitative analysis focuses on all nonfinancial aspects. It provides a background for the financial profile. Qualitative analysis adds value by showing the interrelationship between the numbers and what the numbers mean.

Qualitative analysis requires skills other than simply ticking boxes and calculating scores. In analyzing the qualitative profile of a company, your judgment (or that of your analysts) will make a difference. The world of analyzing is not simple—things are subjective. There is no right or wrong opinion. Evaluating and combining the information brings about the best judgments. Analyzing supplier risks is an investigation. You are given a number of clues, so you must investigate—and then combine—these clues to give better evaluations. This is the case not only in qualitative analysis but also in quantitative analysis. Chapter 5 presents qualitative factors at the macro- and microlevel, such as company environment and company.

Environment

Customers, suppliers, and competitors belong to the environment of a company. Naturally, the position of the company depends on its customers and their success. If the companies that supply your company are small, you might have a counterpart risk if those suppliers fail to deliver. If the subsupplier fails, your deliveries might fail too.

The market situation dictates the guidelines of the business. It is difficult to remain profitable during a market slowdown when competition is severe.

A country's economic and political environment affects a company. In an unstable country, a company is unable get a better rating than its country. In an unstable environment, even a highly rated company faces difficulties.

Company and Management

This component provides the company's profile. The analysis concentrates on company strategy, owners, and management. A strong and logical strategy is a key factor for success. Strong owners provide a strong foundation for a company's success. A strong, committed owner can support a company through difficult times. The quality of management is essential when considering the strengths and weaknesses of a company. Good management plays an important role in the company's internal strengths and possibilities.

3.3 Executive Summary

Corporate analysis starts with the executive summary, including all significant items that affect a company's performance. The executive summary can include the strengths, weaknesses, opportunities, and threats (SWOT) analysis of the company as well as comments and recommendations.

Strengths
: *Positive internal abilities and situations that might enable the company to possess a strategic advantage in achieving objectives.* Strengths provide a company with advantages.

Weaknesses
: *Internal abilities and situations that might result in a company's failure to achieve its objectives.* Weaknesses create disadvantages for a company.

Opportunities
: *Favorable external factors and situations that can assist the company in achieving its objectives.* Opportunities extend the company's possibilities.

Threats
: *Unfavorable characteristics in the company's long-term operating environment.* Threats bring uncertainty.

Recommendations

Recommendations are based on the findings from the quantitative and qualitative components of a corporate analysis and the significance of the supplier. The difference comes from the importance of the supplier to your company. The supplier may be recommended as a supplier in one case but not in another; for example, the supplier could be recommended for standard items but not recommended for long-term cooperation.

Risk Rating

Risk rating is based on the interrelationship between the qualitative and quantitative factors. The remarks and findings are essential in evaluating a company's position.

The rating can be based on the following facts:

❑ *Your (analyst's) subjective judgments.* Where you (the analyst) can rely on experience and knowledge of analyzing large numbers of suppliers in the same industry. It means you can judge the interrelationship and obtain the findings.

❑ *Numeric scoring.* Scores are given to quantitative factors such as growth, profitability, liquidity, leverage, and efficiency and to qualitative factors such as environment, company, and forecast. The scoring is used when there are several routine suppliers that are relatively easy to replace with each other; in this case, the easier and more mechanical rating is needed. It would be a waste of resources to conduct a comprehensive analysis of routine suppliers. A quick analysis is needed to verify your supplier's reliability.

Conclusions are the last component in completing a corporate analysis. It is the core of the corporate analysis, including the value-adding information. Your most significant findings are in this component. The interrelationship between the findings and their importance generates the executive summary.

Key Points

Corporate analysis is a comprehensive analysis that creates a picture of your supplier's capability as a company. It answers the question: Is your supplier a solvent and profitable company that will remain in business?

Corporate analysis consists of quantitative and qualitative analysis of the company. Quantitative factors come from financial statements such as the balance sheet, statements of income, cash flow statement, and the calculated key figures based on the financial statements. Forecasting extends the scope of analysis by providing the opportunity to consider the future. Quantitative analysis is discussed further in Chapter 4.

4

Investigating What Is Behind Financial Figures

FINANCIAL FIGURES ARE like the bones of a company. Financial statements show the company's financial status. After recent accounting scandals and the ensuing scandals resulting from creative accounting methods, the relevance of true financial figures was impaired. It is now even more essential to find the truth behind financial figures. Figure 4-1 shows the financial analysis and forecast in a corporate analysis.

This chapter provides you with the basic meaning of financial statements and what conclusions you can make based on your supplier's financial statements and key ratios. Financial statements include the balance sheet, statements of income (also called profit and loss statements), cash flow statements, and pages of notes containing additional information to help you understand the financial statements.

The basic purpose of financial statements is to assist users in evaluating the financial position, profitability, and future prospects of a company. The annual and quarterly statements of all publicly owned companies are easy to access because the financial statements are public information. The main factors of interest are the solvency, profitability, and growth of a business organization. The key figures for calculating solvency, profitability, and growth are presented in Subchapter 4.5.

Solvent businesses have the ability to pay debts as they come

Figure 4-1. Financial analysis and forecast in corporate analysis.

A	EXECUTIVE SUMMARY

B	ENVIRONMENT

C	COMPANY

D	FINANCIAL ANALYSIS
	Financial statements
	Balance sheet
	Statements of income
	Cash flow statement
	Key ratios
	Forecast
	Different accounting standards: IFRS and U.S. GAAP
	Companies in different countries

due. In contrast, insolvent businesses are unable to meet obligations as they fall due. If your supplier cannot meet its obligations to its suppliers and creditors, it can be assumed that the supplier will have difficulties in fulfilling its commitments to you.

Solvency is critical to the very survival of a business organization. A business that becomes insolvent may be forced into bankruptcy by its creditors. Once bankrupt, a business may be forced to downsize operations, sell its assets, and shut down its facilities. (See the explanation of Chapter 11 in the Glossary.) Credit ratings reflect the solvency of a company. Solvency has a substantial impact on credit ratings given by organizations such as Standard & Poor's, Moody's, and Fitch. A high credit rating helps a company to borrow money more easily at lower margins. Detailed information about credit ratings is presented in the Appendix.

A company needs investors to fund its operations. Investors are interested in the solvency of a business organization, but they are even more interested in its *profitability*. Profitable operations increase the bottom line in a statement of income and, consequently, the value of the shareholders' equity in the balance sheet. A company that continually operates unprofitably will exhaust its resources and be forced out of business. Therefore, you (or the analyst) must study financial statements carefully for clues to the company's solvency and future profitability.

In the short run, solvency and profitability can be independent of each other. A company may operate unprofitably during a given year, yet have enough cash to pay its bills. The strong cash and cash equivalents, additional loans or a public offering, helps the company to remain solvent. A business may be operating profitably, but nevertheless run out of cash by investing heavily. The result is insolvency.

Over the longer term, solvency and profitability go hand in hand. Only profitable and solvent companies can survive. Investors are investing to realize a profit. If your supplier generates a loss in the longer term, its existence is in danger.

One key indicator in the evaluation of short-term solvency is the relationship between *liquid* assets (cash and cash equivalents) and the liabilities requiring payment *in the near future* (accounts payable). By studying the nature of a company's assets, and the amounts and due dates of its liabilities, it is possible to anticipate whether the company is likely to have difficulty in meeting its future obligations. Evaluating long-term solvency is more complicated and involves many other factors.

Companies use different types of accounting standards in different countries. But all accounting standards place companies on a uniform, comparable scale. The commonly known standards are the United States' Generally Accepted Accounting Principles (GAAP), International Financial Reporting Standards (IFRS), and the United Kingdom's GAAP. Financial reporting relies on fundamental principles to provide the general framework for determining what information is included in financial statements, and how this information is presented. Accounting standards of different countries are discussed in Subchapter 4.7.

Consolidated Financial Statements

The consolidated financial statements consist of the accounts and transactions of the company and its majority-owned subsidiaries. Consolidation eliminates intercompany transactions, such as the accounts receivable and accounts payable among the companies. The parent company controls the subsidiaries that are majority owned by the parent company.

In studying financial statements, the accompanying notes and the auditor's report provide useful information. The auditor's report is the approval of the financial statements.

4.1 Audits and Annual Reports

A financial audit is an examination of a company's financial statements performed by a firm of certified public accountants. The purpose of the audit is to provide people outside the organization with an independent expert's opinion as to whether the financial statements constitute a fair presentation.

An auditor's role is independent of the company issuing the financial statement. Because management prepares its own financial statements and reports on the results of its own activities, the auditor's role is to assure the outside world that a complete and reliable picture of the company's financial position and operating results has been produced. Auditors typically do not go through all the books, but select only a sample; a full audit can be very costly. An auditor examines the financial statements and expresses an opinion as to whether those statements were prepared using acceptable accounting and reporting practices and are fairly presented. The report completed by an auditor is called an auditor's report and accompanies the financial statements. An auditor must be independent of the company's management; for example, if the wife of the managing director is the auditor, the report won't have creditability.

Auditors use the following phrases:

❑ The auditor's report illustrates an *unqualified or "clean" opinion,* meaning that the auditor regards the financial statement as a fair presentation in all material respects and the results of operations, the financial position, and the cash flows for the accounting period in conformity with generally accepted accounting principles. The term *fair presentation* describes financial statements that are complete, unbiased, and in conformity with generally accepted accounting principles.

❑ In some cases, the auditor gives a *qualified opinion,* which indicates that the auditor believes the financial statements are overall fairly presented but a specific item (or set of items within the statement) is not presented in conformity with generally accepted accounting principles or disclosure is inadequate.

❑ An *adverse opinion* means that the auditor has not been able to accept the financial statements because they are not presented in accordance with generally accepted accounting principles.

The remarks of the auditor are always clues that you may need to screen the company and its financial statements more carefully.

Large business organizations prepare annual reports for distribution to investors and all other interested parties. Annual reports enable users to identify trends in the company's performance and financial position. Annual reports include (1) top management's summary of the company's financial position, profitability, and future prospects; (2) audited financial statements of two or more years; (3) the auditor's report on the comparative statements; and (4) sections on the different businesses and an overview of those businesses. Nowadays, some companies produce annual reports mainly in electronic format. You can find annual reports on a company's Web site, particularly if the company is listed on a stock exchange.

4.2 Balance Sheet

A balance sheet (also known as the statement of financial position) is a financial "snapshot," taken at a stated point in time, of all assets owned by a company and all claims against those assets. It shows the financial position of the company on a specific date. A balance sheet is a static document showing historical cost. The snapshot can be taken at different times, and the difference between those times is easy to recognize. The snapshots can show trends. Balance sheets can be seen as a statement of source and use of funds, as shown in Figure 4-2. The basic relationship is as follows:

Assets = Liabilities + Shareholders' Equity

Shareholders' equity will be a negative amount if the business has liabilities in excess of its assets. Negative equity is a clear sign of financial difficulties.

The assets can be seen as a list of items and their monetary value to the company. It is easy to see where the funds come from (liabilities and shareholders' equity) and where the funds go (assets). The use of funds must balance with the source of funds.

Figure 4-2. Balance sheet—source and use of funds.

Assets

Liabilities

USES OF FUNDS

- The items that the business owns, i.e., possessions with monetary value

SOURCES OF FUNDS

- Debts and the funds the business owes, i.e., external and internal liabilities

Next, the structure of the balance sheet will be examined in more detail: what components make up assets and liabilities and what components are included in shareholders' equity.

4.2.1 Balance Sheet Structure

Both the assets and liabilities are listed in decreasing order of liquidity. (See Figure 4-3.) The financial structure is in balance if the short-term and long-term commitments are in balance. In practice, this means that current liabilities should be paid by current assets and fixed assets should be paid by shareholders' equity and noncurrent liabilities.

Figure 4-3. Balance sheet—liquidity of balance sheet items.

BALANCE SHEET

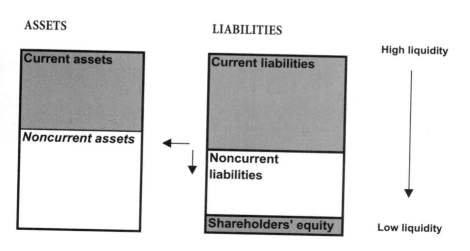

ASSETS   LIABILITIES

Current assets   Current liabilities   High liquidity

Noncurrent assets   Noncurrent liabilities

                          Shareholders' equity   Low liquidity

Classification of Assets

Assets consist of two parts: current assets and noncurrent assets. Current assets are short-lived assets that normally convert into cash within one year. Noncurrent assets are long-lived assets that cannot be realized in cash during the fiscal year. Both current assets and noncurrent assets include several components.

Current Assets

Current assets include cash and cash equivalents, short-term investments, receivables, inventories, and prepaid expenses; these are all expected to be sold or consumed during the fiscal year. Current assets are more liquid in nature than noncurrent assets. Figure 4-4 shows the classification of current assets:

A. *Cash and cash equivalents* include cash on hand, consisting of short-term deposits in a bank and other highly liquid investments. Cash must be available for withdrawal on demand. Cash and cash equivalents show the amount of liquid funds the company has at the closing date of the balance sheet.

B. *Short-term investments* consist of marketable securities that can be sold on short notice to meet current cash needs. Short-term investments must mature within one year.

Figure 4-4. Balance sheet—classification of current assets.

Current assets	Contents
• Cash and cash equivalents	• Cash on hand, short-term deposits in a bank and other highly liquid investments
• Short-term investments	• Marketable securities
• Receivables	• Accounts receivable, notes receivable, and receivables from affiliated companies
• Inventories	• Finished goods, work in process, and raw materials
• Prepaid expenses	• Prepaid rents, prepaid insurances, etc.

C. *Receivables* include several items; the largest portion of receivables is typically accounts receivable. Other receivables include notes receivable and receivables from affiliate companies. Accounts receivable are also called *trade debtors* and *debtors* in the United Kingdom. Accounts receivable are those amounts due from customers from normal business transactions. The unpaid bills of the company's customers make up the bulk of receivables.

A company can collect its accounts receivable in the following ways:

1. It can collect accounts receivable itself.
2. Another alternative is to sell its assets to financial institutions through *factoring* or *securitization of accounts receivable*. When receivables are factored, they are sold to the lender at a discount. This discount can be substantial and any upside (better collections) accrue to the lender. Under the receivable securitization program, the receivable acts as collateral for the lender, but ownership remains with the company. In this case, all collections above the loan remain with the company. The cost of securitization of accounts receivable is generally lower than in factoring.

D. *Inventories* may consist of finished goods, work in process, and raw materials. Inventories are investments that companies must finance. A company has invested funds in the inventory, which causes costs to the company. Because of the cost effect, inventory control is a key area of focus for management.

The term *obsolescence* is often used in conjunction with inventory. Some items in the inventory may become obsolete or out of date and should be written off (see Glossary). An excessive amount of working capital (definition: current assets − current liabilities) can be tied up in an accumulation of needless inventory.

E. *Prepaid expenses* are prepayments made to secure future cash flows. Prepaid expenses include prepaid rent, prepaid insurance, and prepayment of project expenses.

Noncurrent Assets

Noncurrent assets include those assets that are intended to be held for longer than a fiscal year. The following items would be classified as noncurrent assets: (1) long-term investments; (2) property, plant, and equipment; (3) intangible assets; and (4) other assets. Noncurrent assets (the long-lived assets) facilitate the manufacture of products. The accounting value of noncurrent assets is decreased through depreciation. Machinery and equipment need to be replaced at certain times. However, because the company must maintain production, it must invest in new equipment and machinery. It is also possible to lease machinery and equipment. The classification of noncurrent assets is shown in Figure 4-5.

A. *Long-term investments* are investments intended to be held for longer than one year. The following items belong to long-term investments: (1) stocks in associated companies, bonds, or long-term notes; (2) tangible assets to be held long term; and (3) investments for funds, such as pension funds.

B. *Property, plant, and equipment* have a physical structure, such as land, a building, or a machine. Depreciation is the distinguishing factor between land and depreciable assets. Land and depreciable assets can be subdivided into two categories:

1. Depreciation for buildings, which have a useful lifetime

2. Depreciation not taken from land, which has an unlimited term of existence

Figure 4-5. Balance sheet—classification of noncurrent assets.

Noncurrent assets	**Contents**
• Long-term investments	• Investments for funds
• Property, plant, and equipment	• Land, buildings, plant, and equipment
• Intangible assets	• Goodwill, patents, licenses, trademarks
• Other assets	• Deferred taxes, bond issues costs, long-term prepaid expenses

Depreciation

The term *depreciation* is used when the initial cost of a fixed asset, such as tangible property or machinery and equipment, is spread over an appropriate number of accounting periods, that is, in the period in which services are received from the asset. If all the original costs of the fixed assets were charged in full against the period in which they were purchased, a company would presumably show extensive losses in statements of income and would therefore lose its shareholders' equity in the balance sheet.

Depreciation differs from most other expenses because it does not depend on cash payments at or near the time when the expense is recorded. This characteristic of depreciation makes it a "noncash" expense. Depreciation is a process of cost allocation.

C. *Intangible assets* do not have a physical structure; that is, they are nonmaterial assets such as legal rights and acquired goodwill, which are expected to bring future economic benefits. The term *amortization* is used in connection with intangible assets.

Goodwill shows the difference between the book value of the net assets and the price paid in business in an acquisition. Goodwill comes from acquisitions when one company buys another. If the book value of the acquired business is low and the price paid for the acquired company is high, the goodwill will be high. Goodwill must be written off over a certain period of time.

Some companies have paid huge amounts for goodwill, only to discover that they overestimated the future value of the business in question. The company paid too high a price to acquire the other company. If it becomes apparent that the purchased goodwill does not have real economic value, it should be written off immediately. Goodwill is a noncash item.

Many companies were forced to write off goodwill in their financial statements in recent years. Companies that write off a significant amount of goodwill are admitting that they paid too much for an acquisition or an investment.

Patents, copyrights, and trademarks are granted by a government authority to an individual or organization as acknowledgment of the relevant rights. Patents, copyrights, and trademarks have the common characteristic of being evidenced by contract and having a time span specified by agreement or status.

Amortization

The term *amortization* means the reduction in book value of an intangible asset, such as a patent, copyright, trademark, license, franchise, or goodwill, over the period of ownership. Another definition of amortization is the paying back of a loan in a series of installments.

Note: Depreciation and amortization are also in the statements of income. Please consider the connection between depreciation and amortization in the balance sheet and in the income statement.

D. *Other assets.* All other long-lived assets that do not fit within the other noncurrent categories are included in this category. Other assets include items such as deferred taxes, bond issue costs, and long-term prepaid expenses.

4.2.2 Liabilities and Shareholders' Equity

Liabilities and short-term liabilities are the company's financial obligations to external and internal parties. These consist of three parts: (1) current liabilities, (2) noncurrent liabilities, and (3) shareholders' equity. Liabilities are debts owed to a creditor, which can be an organization or a person. Shareholders' equity is a liability to internal parties, that is, to the owners of the company.

Current Liabilities

Current liabilities can be liquidated as current within one year. The liquidation period is relatively short. Current liabilities and current assets are counterparts in liquidity. The classification of short-term liabilities is presented in Figure 4-6.

A. *Short-term borrowings* include bank overdrafts and all other interest-bearing, short-term debts. Notes payable to suppliers and banks, when included in the current category, reflect short-term operating loans.

B. *Current portion of long-term debt* is the portion of the long-term debt that should be amortized during the year. The amortization can be paid by using current assets or debt can be refinanced through another long-term debt.

C. *Accounts payable* is the outstanding payments to suppliers resulting from the company's purchase inventory or services on credit. Generally, trade payables account for the biggest share of ac-

Figure 4-6. Balance sheet—classification of short-term liabilities.

Current liabilities

- Short-term borrowings

- Current portion of long-term debt

- Accounts payable

- Accrued expenses and other liabilities

- Accrued and deferred income tax

- Other current liabilities

Contents

- Notes payable and advances and deposits payable

- Amortization of a long-term debt during the year

- Trade payables

- Wages and salaries payable, benefits payable, interest payable

- Taxes payable

- Dividends payable

counts payable. On average, they are paid within thirty to sixty days.

D. *Accrued expenses and other liabilities* are advances and deposits, which are collections of cash or other assets to ensure the delivery of goods or services in the next fiscal year. Items in this category can include management fees collected but not yet earned, or a customer's prepayment for products manufactured. The amounts collected from customers in advance represent liabilities. Employee salaries and interest on borrowed money are examples of accrued expenses. They are accumulated every day, but they are not paid daily. Employee tax withholdings and sales taxes can also be included in this item.

Dividends can be paid from the aftertax profit. A dividend is a payment to shareholders as a return on investment proportioned to their share ownership. Dividends are supposed to be paid from an operating surplus; however, dividends can be paid without an operating surplus. In this case, a dividend is considered a return on capital. It can be asked why owners should benefit from a company that is generating losses. Note that dividends are not an expense, and they are not deducted from revenue in the income statement. Dividends are not viewed as an expense because these payments do not serve to generate revenue.

E. *Accrued and deferred income tax* includes the amount of unpaid tax the corporation has to pay from its taxable income.

F. *Other current liabilities* include dividends payable to shareholders when declared.

Noncurrent Liabilities

The repayment period of noncurrent liabilities is longer than one year. Long-term loans and debentures are from banks or insurance companies. They are normally secured by mortgages on the company's assets, such as land and buildings financed by long-term loans. The classification of noncurrent liabilities is shown in Figure 4-7.

A. *Long-term liabilities* includes notes and bonds that will take longer than one year to be paid back.

B. *Other long-term liabilities* are items such as lease obligations on equipment and buildings, long-term obligations for future retirement obligations, contingent obligations such as unsettled lawsuits that may have an effect on the future, and agreements to repurchase an asset.

Shareholders' Equity

The owners of a corporation are called *stockholders* or *shareholders*. The owners' equity in a corporation is called *stockholders' equity* or *shareholders' equity*. The classification of shareholders' equity is presented in Figure 4-8.

Figure 4-7. Balance sheet—classification of long-term liabilities.

Noncurrent liabilities	Contents
• Long-term liabilities	• Notes and bonds payable over a longer period than a year
• Other long-term liabilities	• Lease obligations, pension obligations, long-term obligations from retirement, unsettled lawsuits

Figure 4-8. Balance sheet—classification of shareholders' equity.

Shareholders' equity | Contents

Shareholders' equity	Contents
• Preferred stock	• Certain rights superior to common shareholders; preferences to earnings
• Common stock	• Traditional rights over ownership; the right to vote
• Additional paid-in capital	• Difference between issue price and par/stated value or paid-in capital in transactions such as treasury stock, retirement of stock
• Retained earnings	• Cumulative earnings from previous accounting periods
• Accumulated other comprehensive losses	• Treasury stocks

Shareholders' Equity Includes Two Components:

1. Paid-in capital, that is, contributed capital such as capital stock and additional paid-in capital
2. Retained earnings or losses

Capital Stock

Capital stock shows the amount the owners of the company have invested in the business. The basic type of capital stock issued by every corporation is called *common stock.* Large corporations often issue two types of capital stock: common and preferred. Every corporation has common stock, and some corporations also have one or more types of preferred stock:

A. Common stock possesses the traditional rights of ownership— voting rights in corporate matters, participation in dividends, and a residual claim to assets in the event of liquidation.

B. Preferred stock gives shareholders certain preferences over common shareholders.

Most preferred shares have the following distinctive features:

1. Preference to corporate profits before profits can be distributed to common shareholders

2. Right to receive assets before common shareholders in the event the company is liquidated

3. Possible restriction of right to vote to common shareholders

C. *Additional paid-in capital.* Additional paid-in capital shows the amount by which the original sales prices of shares sold exceed the par value of the stock or paid-in capital in transactions such as treasury stock and retirement of stock.

D. *Retained earnings (accumulated profit or loss).* Retained earnings are also called profit and loss from previous years or accumulated profit or loss. Retained earnings from previous years is the shareholders' equity, which has accumulated through profitable operation of the business. Retained earnings are not paid out in the form of dividends. It is important to find the reason why a company is accumulating losses.

E. *Accumulated other comprehensive losses* includes cumulative earnings and losses from previous years and treasury stocks, shares of the company that have been issued, repurchased by the company, and retired or canceled.

Changes in Shareholders' Equity

Shareholders' equity increases in two ways:

1. Investments by the owners

2. Earnings from profitable operation of the business

The increase in shareholders' equity affects positively the financial strength of the company.

Shareholders' equity decreases in connection with the following business operations:

❑ Distribution of cash or other assets by the business to its owners, called *dividends*

❑ Losses from unprofitable business

Balance Sheet Definitions

Market Value

Contents: The value of the asset or item in the market.
Shows: The price the buyer is willing to pay to the seller of the item (stock) at a specific time.

Market Capitalization

Contents: The current share price multiplied by the number of shares outstanding.

Shows: The market value of the company at a specific time.

Book Value

Contents: The value at which assets are reported in the balance sheet.

Shows: The original purchase value of the item less accumulated depreciation. Book value per share is equal to the net assets represented by one share of stock. The term *net assets* means total assets minus total liabilities; in other words, net assets are equal to total shareholders' equity.

Net Worth

Contents: Net worth depends on the validity of the asset values. The definition is the sum of common ordinary shares + all reserves + preferred shares − intangible assets.

Shows: Owner's equity in a business. A decreased or deficit net worth can be attributed to an unprofitable trend and deduction of intangibles because of goodwill, patents, franchises, copyrights, and cost in excess of market value.

Total Assets

Contents: The value of total assets is as follows: current assets + noncurrent assets = current liabilities + noncurrent liabilities + shareholders' equity.

Shows: The size of the business.

Capital Employed

Contents: Capital employed can be determined as follows: current assets + noncurrent assets − current liabilities = shareholders' equity + noncurrent liabilities.

Shows: It can be considered as representative of the long-term foundation funds of the company.

Key Questions

The most significant questions are marked with an asterisk.

Current Assets

❑ What is the level of cash and marketable securities?*

❑ Has cash and marketable securities decreased? Why?*

❑ Is the inventory increasing significantly as a percentage of total assets? The increase might signal involuntary inventory accumulation, that is, buildup resulting from an unanticipated slowdown in sales.

❑ What are the accounts receivable compared to the accounts payable?

If accounts payable are higher than accounts receivable, the company must pay more to its suppliers than it is receiving from its customers at that moment. It may also indicate that the company is effectively collecting its receivables and has advantageous payment terms for its suppliers.

Noncurrent Assets

❑ Have noncurrent assets increased or decreased during the period? Why?*

The change in noncurrent assets shows the investments of the company during the period.

❑ Does the company have goodwill? Should it be written off?*

❑ Does the company own licenses? What is the value of the licenses?

❑ Does the company own patents?

❑ Has the company overinvested in noncurrent assets?*

Current Liabilities

❑ Is the company funding long-term investments with current liabilities?*

❑ Is it possible? If not, why is the company not seeking long-term financing?

❑ Is working capital increasing or decreasing? Why?

❑ Does the company have high indebtedness? If so, monitor the trend in current and noncurrent liabilities.

Noncurrent Liabilities

❑ What is the level of current liabilities compared with noncurrent liabilities?

❑ Does bank financing exist, or does the company use cash from internally generated funds to finance its operations?

If the current liabilities are high, the company may be financed by paying suppliers slowly. Suppliers do not like providing this type of financing, and they will normally shorten the payment terms for those customers. If bank financing does not exist, consider whether the company is possibly considered a risk company to the banking community.

Shareholders' Equity

❑ If new cash comes into the business as the result of an initial public offering (IPO) or recapitalization, how does it impact the balance sheet? Does the company pay back its long-term loans?

Repayments are part of normal business. If the company does not amortize its loans, what is it doing with the new funds? Are the funds going toward new investments?

❑ Does slow payment to suppliers continue to exist, even with the infusion of additional cash? Presumably, the company is in deep trouble if it continually pays its suppliers late.

Balance Sheet

Issues for Special Attention

❑ Remember that the balance sheet shows a financial snapshot at a specific moment. It does not necessarily show the current situation.

❑ Check for changes in cash and marketable securities. If cash and marketable securities are decreasing, the company may run out of cash. A company can convert cash to marketable securities to get a better return on funds, or it can sell marketable securities to increase cash. Marketable securities are short-term deposits and other liquid securities.

❑ Show caution if a company has high accounts payable and slow turnover. This indicates that the company is using other suppliers to finance operations. A warning flag should go up especially when no bank funding exists and accounts payable are excessive or turnover is slow. It is possible that no bank is willing to lend to the company. The reason for the generosity of suppliers or delayed payments on the part of the company should be identified.

❑ Be concerned if the external liabilities are excessive. This situation might indicate that the company is a risk to the banking community in a time of rising interest rates. It is an indicator of a weak cash flow and a high probability of financial risk that could result in bankruptcy.

❑ Take note if the company is in default of the credit agreement; for example, check whether loan covenants impose restrictions or shareholders' equity. In default, the financial situation is already serious.

❑ Look out for highly leveraged conditions (significant amount of loans compared to shareholders' equity) and whether sales are down and the condition is unprofitable. The company might have difficulty in finding financiers.

❑ Consider the explanations as to why the company delays its payments to its suppliers.

❑ Take note if goodwill is high and there are no signs of amortizing it in a downhill market. The company is possibly showing results that are too positive.

❑ Consider the explanations when accounts payable turnover does not improve, yet cash flow has improved. Be concerned if the turnover remains unchanged or increases, because this may be an indication that cash flow is being diverted for other uses than for business, for example, in some cases to benefit the owner's other business.

4.3 Statements of Income

The statement of income shows the total revenue earned and the total costs incurred over an accounting period. Whereas the balance sheet is a snapshot reflecting specific moments of time, the statement of income (also called a profit and loss statement) is a link between the opening and closing balance sheet of an accounting period. (See Figure 4-9.) A twelve-month accounting period is termed a *fiscal year*. A calendar year is a typical time span for a fiscal year. Other time frames are also used; for example, in Japan the fiscal year ends at the end of March.

Figure 4-10 specifies the items that are generally included in statements of income. The specific contents of the statements of income vary slightly depending on the accounting standard used.

Statement of Income Definitions

Revenue is also called net sales and turnover (in Great Britain). The entity has earned the money from goods sold and services rendered during the given accounting period. Revenue is generally recognized in different points, which is discussed in more detail next.

Revenue recognition refers to the point at which revenue is recognized. It is possible to recognize revenue at different points in the production/selling cycle, and the particular point chosen could have a significant effect on the total revenue reported for the period. The first point at which it is possible to recognize revenue occurs when the goods are delivered. International Accounting Standards (IAS) and GAAP regulations guide revenue recognition. It is important to note any changes in the company's policy of recognizing revenue and the effects on the reported revenue.

Cost of goods sold includes the cost of inventory items during the period. A manufacturing company counts items such as the direct

Figure 4-9. Connection between balance sheet and statements of income.

Balance sheet	Statements of Income	Balance sheet
December 31, 2002	Revenues and costs from January 1, 2002, to December 31, 2002, twelve-month fiscal year	December 31, 2003

Figure 4-10. Sample statement of income.

Statement of Income

- Revenues (net sales, turnover)
- Cost of sales
- *Gross profit*

- OPERATING EXPENSES:
  Selling, general, and administrative
  Research and development
  Goodwill amortization costs
  Acquisition costs
  Restructuring and impairment costs
  Operating income (loss)

- Interest income
- Interest expense

- *Income (loss) before income taxes*
- Income taxes (benefit)
- Extraordinary items
- *Net income (loss)*

Gross profit
(margin) the difference between net sales and cost of goods sold

Operating income is gross profit less operating expenses

EBIT = earnings before interest and tax

EBITDA = earnings before interest, tax depreciation, and amortization

materials inventory at the beginning of the period, purchased materials, and the direct materials inventory at the end of the period.

Gross profit (margin) is the difference between revenue and the cost of goods sold.

Operating expenses include operation-related expenses other than the cost of goods sold. Operating expenses have two main categories—(1) selling expenses, and (2) general and administrative expenses—and a third subcategory—other income (expense).

Selling expenses are those that are directly related to sales, such as advertising costs, salaries of sales personnel, or commissions. General and administrative expenses are related to the general administration of the company. The salaries of administrative staff are included in this item as well as office supplies, legal services, postage, and telephone expenses.

The third category includes several possible items, such as research and development (R&D) expenses and goodwill amortization; acquisition costs and restructuring and impairment costs are discussed later.

All these costs are necessary to attract and serve customers and thereby earn revenue.

Costs are incurred when goods are consumed, not when they are purchased or paid for. Those costs related directly to revenue (net sales) are easy to identify. R&D costs are those related to the planned exploration or investigation to discover new knowledge to produce new products or services. R&D costs are those costs associated with carrying out the R&D work including materials, facilities, personnel, and indirect costs attributed to R&D. It is more problematic to place R&D costs and to identify or determine in which accounting period they should be included: The reporting of the costs depends on when the results of the R&D work are used. The method of capitalizing R&D costs significantly affects a company's results.

Depreciation. There are several transactions affecting the revenue for two or more accounting periods. The costs of these assets will be allocated as an expense over a span of several accounting periods by making adjusting entries at the end of each accounting period. The term *depreciation* is used for writing off (reducing) fixed assets, such as machinery and equipment. Depreciation is a noncash expense. Depreciation expenses reduce net income but do not require a cash outlay during the period.

The rationale for depreciation lies in the matching principle. The goal is to offset a reasonable portion of the asset's cost against revenue in each period of the asset's useful life. The appropriate amount of depreciation expense is only an estimate of the useful lifetime of the asset.

Once the amount to be depreciated has been estimated, the method for allocating the depreciation should be selected. There are two methods of depreciation that are typically used:

1. *Straight-line method.* An equal amount of depreciation is charged for each year the asset is held.

2. *Reducing balances method.* A fixed percentage rate of depreciation to the written-down value of an asset is reduced each year.

Amortization means the reduction in book value of an intangible asset, specifically patents, copyrights, trademarks, licenses, franchises, and goodwill, over the period owned. Depreciation and amortization are also explained in Subchapter 4.2.1.

The first section on statements of income contains only the results of *continuing business activities*. Profit from continuing operations measures the profitability of the ongoing operations. Discontinued operations are those that are sold or discontinued in the accounting period. Extraordinary items are of an unusual nature; the underlying event is abnormal and the occurrence is infrequent.

Acquisition costs primarily relate to any acquisitions made by the company. Acquisitions costs consist of investment banker fees, legal fees, accounting fees, and other direct costs associated with the company's acquisition or acquisitions.

Restructuring and impairment costs. The downsizing of a business causes restructuring costs or charges. The reason for downsizing may be the market-driven cost savings, strategic refocusing on more profitable businesses (to core business), or a company restructuring due to mergers and acquisitions. In practice, recharging costs are those extra costs the company incurs to organize its business, for example, losses on write-downs or sales of plant assets, severance pay to terminated workers, and expenses related to relocation of operations and remaining personnel. Restructuring should not be done as a result of continued collapse or loss, but because the continuation of certain operations is not consistent with profit and growth expectations or because they do not "fit" with the company's other businesses.

Restructuring charges to reorganize a company are considered as onetime, nonrecurring expenses, and "unusual" in nature. However, some companies have used restructuring charges to manipulate their operating results in their favor. Be aware if the company is using restructuring items on a regular basis or a onetime basis. If restructuring costs appear on a regular basis on the company's profit and loss statement, they are recurring operating expenses of the company.

The terms *nonrecurring* and *nonoperating* refer to the financial transactions that are not directly connected to the company's business. The transaction will not affect the company's ability to generate future operating profit. The following transactions are nonrecurring and nonoperating in nature:

- ❏ Selling a building; for example, a headquarters or factory building
- ❏ Write-downs for the impairment of assets
- ❏ Extraordinary items

Operating income (loss) (also called earnings before interest and tax, EBIT) shows the profit or loss after reducing all costs related to the operations. Positive cash flow is very important to every company.

Interest income includes interest on notes receivable, bank deposits, government bonds, or other securities.

Interest expense is the cost of borrowing money, for example, in conjunction with a loan or delinquent payments to suppliers. In the latter case, the company is taking a nonnegotiated "loan" from its suppliers. It is easy to take this so-called loan from a supplier; however, over the long run, it results in less favorable payment terms and possibly higher-priced products. Nonnegotiated loans from suppliers can be found on credit reports in the section marked "delays in payment."

A highly leveraged company has a high rate of indebtedness and therefore high interest charges. If a company has low profitability, it may have difficulties paying the interest on its loans, let alone the installments on the principal. This kind of situation cannot last long; external financiers like banks are not pleased to see no payments on principal or interest installments. The company enters into a situation where it is tightly controlled by the bank.

Income (loss) before income taxes. Income before income taxes shows the ability of the company to cover its tax burden with funds earned from operations.

Income taxes. Profitable businesses must file income tax returns and pay income taxes equal to a percentage of their taxable income. These taxes represent an expense for the business organization.

Extraordinary items are those items that are unusual in nature and characteristically infrequent in their occurrence. For example, a loss on early extinguishment of debt can be classified as an extraordinary item.

Net income (loss). Net income is the income that will be shifted to the balance sheet next year, part of which may be allocated to shareholder dividends.

Taxation and Ownership

When analyzing companies and their profit, it is important to remember the effect taxation and ownership has on the companies' profits. Privately and publicly owned companies have different attitudes about sharing profits and taxation. The company's willingness to show profit is based on items such as its legal form. Generally, a publicly owned company looks for opportunities to maximize its net profit, while its financing is dependent on its market value. Investors use profitability and the ability to pay dividends as criteria for valuing the company and its shares. Publicly owned companies use accounting rules to their advantage to maximize net profit.

Rather than minimizing their taxes, privately owned companies often save the funds for future growth. They don't need to impress their shareholders and gain better value for their shares if the company is not for sale.

To understand the "life" of a company, you must understand what the different items in the statement of income mean. The different items show where the company is spending its revenue and whether those items are in accordance with the revenue or the company's spending is higher than its earnings. The importance of the quality of the financial statements can never be overestimated. The analysis cannot exceed the quality of the material on which it is based; that is, a low-quality financial statement will generate a low-quality analysis. You should take into consideration the differences between the pro forma statements and the consolidated and nonconsolidated financial statements.

Consolidated Financial Statements

A series of accounting scandals has severely damaged investors' confidence in financial statements. Some companies have increased suspicion toward so-called true accounts. The suspicions are justified if a company is using nonconsolidated, off balance sheet vehicles, such as the financing of an R&D partnership with another company or allocating nonprofitable investments into another company. In some cases, the names of the companies are very similar. One of those companies may even be publicly listed while the other company is a "wastebasket."

Operating leases, whereby a company agrees to rent an asset over a substantial period of time and make up off balance sheet financing. Try to determine if all special-purpose entities are consolidated into the company's accounts. Auditors should give their opinions and insist that an entity be brought onto the balance sheet. The requirements in accounting standards also come into play.

Key Questions

The most significant questions are marked with an asterisk.

Revenue = Net Sales

❑ What is the level of net sales?

❑ Is the company small, medium, or large?

❑ Have sales decreased during a period of increasing inventory levels?*

If sales are decreasing and inventory is increasing, a company is producing inventory. More working capital is needed to finance the increasing inventory.

Changes in Net Sales Percentage

❑ Has revenue increased or decreased? Why?*

❑ How quick has the growth or decline of net sales been?

❑ What has been the three-year net sales trend?

If net sales have decreased, it is important to determine the reason behind the reduction.

Gross Profit

❑ Is gross profit decreasing during a period of increased sales?*

❑ Is gross profit increasing during a period of decreased sales?

❑ Was gross margin impacted by competition, product pricing, level of sales, and/or inventory valuation?

Operating Expenses

❑ What was the amount of depreciation and amortization?

❑ What was the reason for high depreciation and amortization?

❑ Is the company going to have high depreciation and amortization in the future?

❑ Are administrative expenses and restructuring charges impacting profitability? How much have those changes affected profitability?*

❑ Were the restructuring costs onetime charges, or are these costs expected in the future, too?

❑ Are production costs too high? What is the company going to do to decrease its production costs?

❑ Are personnel costs too high? What is the company going to do to decrease personnel costs?*

❑ Was operating profit impacted by restructuring charges, reorganization, interest expense, or nonrecurring charges? Are these costs expected also in the future? You can calculate operating profit with and without these extra costs to find the real operating profit during that period.*

❑ How much have investments cost? Are the investments too large compared to anticipated future income?*

Operating Income (Loss)

❑ What was the amount of operating income?*

❑ What has been the trend? Has operating profit increased or decreased?

❑ What is the projected operating income for the next two or three years?*

❑ If net sales are increasing, why is operating income decreasing?*

If net sales have increased or decreased, determine what factors impacted the changes.

❑ Is operating income negative or decreasing during a period of increased sales? If so, the company may be dumping its products.*

❑ Were the changes impacted by business strategy, a deteriorating financial condition, economic problems, manufacturing deficiencies, lack of upgraded technologies, or competition?*

❑ What are the loan covenants, for example, a specific earnings before interest, tax, depreciation, and amortization (EBITDA) level?*

❑ What factors affect the positive or negative condition of gross profit and operating profit margin? What are the factors that affected this level of performance?*

Operating Profit Percentage of Net Sales

❑ What percentage of operating profit has been from net sales during the past three years?

It is important to find the trend and the reasons behind the trend.

❑ Has profitability increased or decreased? What was the reason for the change?

❑ What is the expected trend in operating profit as a percentage in the future? Why?

Later you will determine how accurate the company was in making its forecast.

Interest

❑ Does the company have high debts and high interest to pay?*

❑ Does the company's operating profit cover its interest costs? If not, its debt-to-profit ratio is too high.

❑ What are the financing costs? What is the interest rate on any loans?

❑ Is the company paying higher than market interest rates?

❑ Does the company have enough cash to pay its interest costs? How long can the company cover the interest costs?*

Dividends

❑ Has the company paid out dividends even when it recorded an operating loss? If so, why is the company returning capital to its owners?

❑ Do the owners' benefits outweigh the company's ability to generate profit?*

Net Profit/Loss

❑ What was the net profit or loss amount? Why did the company record a profit or loss? What is the expected profit or loss in the future? Why?*

Net Profit Percentage from Net Sales

❑ How much profit did the company make compared to net sales? Has the profit/sales decreased or increased?

❑ Did the company generate a net profit?

Statements of Income—Issues for Special Attention

- ❑ Find out the reasons for a loss. Unprofitable products, excessive operating costs, and deficient management skills for solving problems are serious issues.

- ❑ Be aware of inventory write-downs, or if the company has obsolete inventory or overvalued inventory.

- ❑ Be aware of the possibility of high amortization, depreciation, and restructuring costs after excessive acquisitions, especially if the economic trend takes a turn for the worse.

- ❑ Pay attention if the company pays dividends to its shareholders when it records a loss. A red flag is raised when a company pays considerable dividends to its owners even though it generates a loss. Are the owners trying to cut their losses before the "ship sinks"?

- ❑ Pay attention to explanations of low profitability. Look at all the facts collectively and determine whether the explanation is realistic. There must be a plan to cut costs and to improve profitability.

- ❑ Keep in mind that trends do not go on forever. If a company generates a profit one year, the market situation can change and the company could record a loss the following year, and vice versa.

- ❑ Do not make hasty conclusions by looking at only the bottom line, net profit, or loss. Find out the real financial performance in the period and the reason behind the profit or loss.

4.4 Cash Flow Statement

The cash flow statement is a list of the *source of funds* and the *use of funds*. A cash flow statement summarizes the cash receipts and cash payments of the business over the same time period as the statements of income. The cash flow statement shows how the company generates and uses its cash. Cash flows are classified according to the nature of the underlying business activity. The three activities are operating activities, investing activities, and financing activities.

The main function of the cash flow statement is to show the profitability of business operations. Operating activities should be the main source of cash. A capable company stays in business and generates net income and more cash. Profitability is a significant driver of every organization. A profitable company increases the amount of shareholders' equity through profitable operations; therefore, the owners will be satisfied with the return on their investment. A capable company also satisfies other external groups, such as creditors and other financiers, by settling payments of debts and other obligations as they come due. Good liquidity in a company increases its flexibility in business. A profitable company can go bankrupt if it runs out of short-term cash to deal with trade creditors, particularly when expanding. It is important to notice the difference between operating cash flow and overall cash flow. Also, a company can be cash-flow profitable but loss making, that is, selling assets.

A cash flow statement serves the following purposes:

❑ Finds out the company's solvency through its cash flows: where the money comes from and where it goes

❑ Helps to understand the company through different activities

❑ Provides additional information about certain cash flows not specifically defined on the income statement and balance sheet

❑ Identifies the company's ability to generate positive cash flows

❑ Shows the company's ability to meet its obligations and to pay dividends

❑ Reviews the company's need for external financing

The cash flow includes both cash receipts and cash payments. The classification of cash flows covers three major categories, as mentioned earlier: (1) operating activities, (2) investing activities, and (3) financing activities. Figure 4-11 shows the content of the cash flow statement.

Cash Flows from Operating Activities

For long-term survival, a business must generate a positive net cash flow from its operating activities with customers. If the bulk of the operating cash comes from customers, it is a strong and positive signal. The focus business operations are the main source of cash in a healthy company.

Figure 4-11. Content of cash flow statement.

Cash flow from operating activities:
   a) Cash received from customers
   b) Cash received from interest
   c) Cash paid to suppliers and employees
   d) Cash paid for interest
   e) Cash paid for income taxes
Net cash flow from operating activities

+ Cash flow from investing activities:
   f) Cash paid for capital additions and businesses acquired
   g) Proceeds from divestitures
Net cash flow used for investing activities

+ Cash flow from financing activities:
   h) Proceeds from short-term and long-term debt
   i) Payment of long-term debt
   j) Issuance and/or purchase of treasury stock
   k) Cash dividends paid
Net cash flow used for financing activities
+ Net effect of exchange rate changes on cash
= Net increase (or decrease) in cash

Cash Flows from Investing Activities

Financing is required to purchase equipment and machinery and to acquire businesses. Investments and purchases create cash outflows. By contrast, selling equipment, machinery, buildings, or a part of the business creates cash inflows. A company that is generating losses can increase its cash by selling its assets.

Cash Flows from Financing Activities

This item shows the short-term and long-term borrowing during a year. Increasing long-term debt and issuing stocks increases cash.

Cash flow statements also show whether the company pays dividends.

One of the signs of a successful business is the regular payment of dividends. In the absence of other financing transactions, dividend payments cause many companies to incur negative net cash flows from their financing activities. It is important to recognize the payments of dividends and their effect on net cash flows.

Source and Use of Cash

A company generates and uses cash in several different ways. Some of the actions to increase and decrease cash are listed next. Over an accounting period, the use of funds must equal the source of funds.

Actions for Generating Cash Include:

❑ Increase shareholders' equity by a public offering.
❑ Add liabilities by taking loans from banks or other financial institutions.
❑ Sell assets such as plants, headquarters building, and/or unnecessary equipment.
❑ Accelerate receivables rotation.

Actions for Reducing Cash Include:

❑ Purchase plants, buildings, machinery, and/or equipment.
❑ Increase assets by growing inventory and/or by slowing turnover of accounts receivable or growth of sales.
❑ Reduce liabilities by accelerating payments to suppliers.

Key Questions

The most significant questions are marked with an asterisk.

❑ Is cash flow greater than debt service? This condition shows whether the company is capable of repaying its debts.*

If a company is not capable of repaying debts, it can possibly refinance them. If refinancing is not possible and the company cannot repay the loans that are due, the company is in deep trouble.

❑ Is the company able to generate cash from operating activities?*

A start-up company can be cash negative. If a going concern (a business with a longer business history) has a negative cash flow, the restructuring of operations might be needed.

❑ How is the company financing its activities?*

If current and noncurrent liabilities are increasing quickly, keep a close watch on the situation. Quickly rising debt is an alarming sign of difficulties.

4.5 Key Ratios

This subchapter addresses the contents and meaning of the financial ratios, here called *key ratios*. The formats of how to calculate the performance ratios are presented first. Then, there is a selection of typical questions related to key ratios to help you understand your findings and the relationship between the findings.

After examining the structure and analyzing historical financial statements, it is time to take a closer look at the calculations and the analysis of the financial ratios. This evaluation is made to measure the financial performance of your supplier and to help you understand the direction of development.

Financial ratios provide a quick and relatively simple means of examining the financial health of a business. A ratio is a comparison of figures in financial statements. By calculating a relatively small number of key ratios it is often possible to create a reasonably good picture of a company's position and performance.

Financial numbers and ratios differ according to different business segments—that is, engineering from electronics. The key ratios should be compared within individual segments. It is a useful tool for benchmarking a company against both its rating and its peers. The ability to understand relative performance benchmarking of similar segment industries helps to reveal the real efficiency of the target business.

These figures have been chosen from a large selection of possible financial figures to keep the supplier analysis as simple and effective as possible. Understanding the financial key ratios is an essential part of analyzing companies. The results of these quantitative, measurable analyses should be reviewed, along with the financial statement, to obtain a better understanding of a company's financial standing.

The key figures are categorized into six different groups to find all possible aspects of a company's development. The six groups are:

1. Growth
2. Profitability
3. Efficiency
4. Liquidity
5. Leverage
6. Investment

It is essential to remember that the significance of any financial measurement depends on two factors: (1) trend over time; and (2) relationship to industry averages, or measurement within similar companies. By comparing the financial figures of companies in the same industry, you can find differences among the companies. A company might show better ratios than its competitors. The trend of key ratios over time is different. Because the management of those companies made different decisions during those times, the resources of those companies vary.

Ratios provide a quick and useful method for analyzing the position and performance of a business. Because ratio analysis has limitations such as quality, scope, and time, it cannot provide the exact truth about a company's performance. Ratio analysis has limitations and problems that should be taken into consideration, such as:

The *quality of the analysis* is limited by the quality of the financial statements. The first and most important factor is the quality of the financial statements. If the financial statements are creative, the key ratios cannot exceed the quality of the underlying financial statements.

The *scope of analysis* is enlarged by other information in the financial statements. Notes provide additional information to increase the understanding of financial ratios. Ratios provide only a restricted vision of financial statements. Therefore, it is important to not rely exclusively on ratios. Ratios cannot provide an explanation of the specific figures.

The *time scale* is limited in history. A statement of income (profit and loss statement) shows a specific period of time, but a balance sheet is only a snapshot of a specific time. Balance sheet ratios are based on a specific time. Any ratios based on balance sheet figures, such as liquidity ratios, may not be representative of the financial position of the business for the year as a whole. You must remember the time limit. A weak financial position six months ago may have deteriorated even further, or it may have improved.

Definitions and Formulas

Growth

❑ Growth ratios reveal the trend of the business.

Net Sales Change

Formula

$$\frac{(\text{Net Sales Y2} - \text{Net Sales Y1})}{\text{Net Sales Y1}}$$

Percentage change = The rate at which an amount is increasing or decreasing.

Definition

Net sales can also be called revenue and turnover. When comparing the changes in the first year (Y1) with changes in the second year (Y2), measure the change in net sales. Therefore, the change is the result of certain factors. It is important to learn the reasons behind the change, especially when net sales are decreasing.

Summary

❑ Growth that occurs too quickly casts fear about current and future profitability.

❑ Growth that is too slow indicates difficulties in a declining industry.

Profitability

❑ Profitability ratios indicate how efficiently the company is using its assets. Profitability ratios show the success of the business and its ability to create wealth for its owners.

Profitability is the company's ability to translate sales into profits.

Before defining gross margin, we are going to divide the costs between variable and fixed costs in the statement of income. The level of sales affects variable costs. Fixed costs are not dependent on sales. Variable costs include, for example, material costs and variable wages and salaries. These costs vary based on the volume of activity. Fixed monthly salaries and rents for premises are examples of fixed costs. A company is less flexible if it has a high proportion of fixed costs; therefore, if sales decline, a company cannot easily adapt its costs to the new level of sales.

Gross Margin Percentage

Formula

$$\frac{\text{Gross margin}}{\text{Net sales}}$$

Definition

Gross profit (margin) measures the profitability of the company's products. Gross profit is the first step in measuring the company's profitability on the statement of income. Gross profit and operating profit margin measure overall efficiency and performance.

Summary

❏ Gross profit that is too low can create troubles in the future.

Operating Income Margin

Formula

$$\frac{\text{Operating income}}{\text{Net sales}}$$

Definition

The second step in measuring profitability is reviewing operating income (operating profit). Operating income shows the profit after the fixed and variable costs that are required to conduct business. When analyzing a company, it is essential to find out the reasons behind a change in operating income and net sales. Operating income margin varies among different business areas. Companies concentrating on production are the most cost intensive, so the operating margin is typically low in businesses like electronic manufacturing services (EMS).

Operating income/sales exclude the effects of investments (income from affiliates or assets sales), financing (interest expense), and tax position. If the operating margin is low or even negative, a company cannot pay interest and taxes with the funds received through its operations. The operating margin should be positive, at least during certain years. Normally, a start-up company generates an operating loss during its first years of existence.

Summary

❏ An operating margin that is too low could indicate that the company will not survive long in the business.

❏ An operating margin that is too high compared with its competitors' in a downhill market raises the question: Has the company reported all costs?

Return on Assets

Formula

$$\frac{\text{Net income}}{\text{Total assets (average)}}$$

As a key indicator of profitability for a company, this ratio shows whether management has earned a reasonable return on assets. It matches net income with assets available to earn a return. Companies efficiently using their assets will have a relatively high return, while unprofitable businesses will have relatively low return.

The return on assets (ROA) should be higher than the interest paid; otherwise the company's cost of borrowing is higher than the return on assets. There is no sense in lending to an unprofitable business. A successful business might earn a return on assets of 13 to 16 percent, if the interest rate to borrow capital is between 4 and 8 percent.

Summary

❏ An ROA that is too low shows poor use of assets.

❏ An ROA that is too high raises the question: How can the company run its business with low assets?

Return on Equity

Formula

$$\frac{\text{Net income}}{\text{Total shareholders' equity (average)}}$$

Definition

Shareholders' equity = Paid-in capital and retained earnings or losses

Return on equity (ROE) is an essential ratio for investors to measure the return on their investments. ROE measures the efficiency with which the company employs owners' capital. The higher the return on equity, the more pleased the stockholder will be. ROE reveals how profitable an investment your supplier is to its owners.

Summary

❑ An ROE that is too low might indicate a fear of bankruptcy.
❑ An ROE that is too high might show low investments by owners.

Net Asset Turnover

Formula

$$\frac{\text{Net sales}}{\text{Net assets (average)}}$$

Net assets = Total assets − (current liabilities + noncurrent liabilities) = Net worth

Definition

Net asset turnover measures how efficient the company's management has been in generating sales from the operating assets at its disposal. Net asset turnover shows the number of times the net asset is turned over by the net sales for a period. A higher figure indicates a more efficient use of capital. A high ratio could indicate that the company will generate further business without an increase in invested capital.

Summary

❏ A net asset turnover that is too low shows poor management of assets.

Efficiency or Activity Ratios

❏ Efficiency ratios measure the efficiency with which certain resources have been utilized within the business.

Collection Period

This refers to the debtor's collection period or to accounts receivable (A/R) turnover days.

Formulas

Accounts Receivable Turnover

$$\frac{\text{Net sales}}{\text{Average accounts receivable}} = \text{X times}$$

Average Number of Days to Collect Accounts Receivable

$$\frac{\text{Days in years}}{\text{Accounts receivable turnover}} = \frac{365}{\text{X times}} = \text{Y days}$$

The collection period controls the efficiency of the company's management of accounts receivable. Accounts receivable (debtor's) is divided by the net sales per days in the accounting period. If the collection period is an average of forty days, the company is receiving cash after the sale relatively quickly. If the average collection period is 120 days, the company has granted long terms of payments to its customers, or some customers are unable to make payments or are having difficulty in doing so. If the collection period is long, it is important to check the reason behind it as well as the trend of the collection period. In general, an accounts receivable collection period of fifty days or less is optimal.

Summary

❏ An accounts receivable ratio that is too slow may cause short-term financial problems because the company has to finance its customers.

Payable Period (Creditors' Turnover Period)

Formula

$$\frac{\text{Accounts payable}}{\text{Cost of goods sold}} \times 365 = Y \text{ days}$$

Definition

Accounts payable can also be called *creditors*. The payable period is the opposite of the collection period. It measures the speed at which payables are paid, and it reflects the liability of a company. The payable period is divided by the cost of goods sold during the accounting period. An average ninety-day payable period shows that the company will pay its suppliers in ninety days. If the average terms of payment with the suppliers are thirty days, the company is paying its suppliers somewhat later than average. The manner of payment varies from country to country. In some countries, delays are more serious than in other countries.

Summary

❑ A payment period that is too long can affect deliveries.

❑ A payment period that is too short could indicate financial difficulties in a company. Its suppliers are selling by cash only.

Inventory Turnover

Inventory turnover is also referred to as the stock turnover ratio.

Formula

$$\frac{\text{Cost of goods sold}}{\text{Inventory (average)}} = X \text{ times}$$

(Average inventory = Beginning inventory + Ending inventory)/2

Definition

If both the opening and closing inventory are available, the average inventory (stock) should be used in order to obtain a more accurate picture of inventory turnover. The average inventory is half of the sum of opening and closing inventory.

This ratio reflects how many times the company's inventory

turns per year—that is, how quickly inventory is sold. A high inventory turnover is often regarded as a sign of efficiency. If the inventory turns over three times, it means that on average items stay in inventory almost four months (12 months/3 times = 4 months). The slower the inventory turnover, the more funds that are needed to finance the inventory. Check the status of inventory as accurately as you can: If inventory turnover is very slow, it is possible that the company has obsolete inventory. A slow inventory turnover along with decreasing sales is an alarming combination.

Inventory turnover depends on the industry in which the company operates. Service companies should not have any inventory. Generally speaking, an inventory turnover of fifty days or less is good. However, keep in mind that inventory turnover varies from industry to industry.

Summary

❑ Too little inventory can cause stock-outs and lost sales.

❑ Too high an inventory could indicate poor inventory management, surplus inventory, or obsolete inventory.

Liquidity

Liquidity ratios measure how quickly an item can be converted to cash. A company should meet its cash obligations when they fall due; otherwise, the company can develop creditor problems.

Current Ratio

Formula

$$\frac{\text{Current assets}}{\text{Current liabilities}}$$

Definition

The current ratio indicates short-term solvency. It shows creditors the borrower's ability to pay its current liabilities. Current assets are assets that can be converted into cash within a year, whereas current liabilities are liabilities that must be paid within a year. Inventories are included in the current ratio. The time perspective is slightly longer in current ratio than in quick ratio (formula: current assets −

inventory − prepaid expenses)/current liabilities due to the expectation that inventories and assets can be realized in order to handle short-term liabilities. It is possible that a company could have a favorable current ratio yet be unable to meet current liabilities because of nonliquid, surplus inventory. A company with a low current ratio has poor liquidity.

The quick ratio, accounts receivable, and inventory turnover should be analyzed in conjunction with the current ratio to determine the overall liquidity position. The trend and combination of these figures provides a more reliable picture of the liquidity position. Table 4-1 shows some meanings of current ratio levels. In general, the current ratio depends on the company's industry.

Table 4-1. Current ratio.

Current ratio	Indication of the meaning
>2	Excellent, strong short-term financial position
1.5–1.9	Good
1.0–1.4	Satisfactory
<1.0	Weak

A company with a strong cash flow can operate successfully with a lower current ratio level than a company with a weaker cash flow. If the current ratio is low, a company must pay higher margins to borrow money.

Generally, the higher the company's current ratio, the stronger its financial position. A high current ratio maintains a comfortable working capital. Notice that a high current and quick ratio can also show inefficient use of current assets. The reasons might be (1) there is a surplus inventory, (2) debtors are taking or have been granted extended credit, or (3) cash is not put to effective use. Cash can earn poorly in a bank account.

You should pay attention if the current ratio and quick ratio stay high for a long period of time.

Summary

❑ A current ratio that is too high could indicate that the company is holding excessive cash, accounts receivable, or inventory. Capital is not being used productively in the business. Management needs to pay more attention to the use of current assets.

❏ A current ratio that is too low could indicate poor ability to satisfy short-term obligations. The result might be financing problems in the short term.

Acid test ratio = *Quick ratio*

Formulas

$$\frac{(Current\ assets\ -\ inventory)}{Current\ liabilities}$$

Also to be determined:

$$\frac{(Cash\ +\ short\text{-}term\ investments\ +\ net\ current\ receivables)}{Current\ liabilities}$$

Definition

The highly liquid current assets (cash, marketable securities, and receivables) are called *quick assets*. The ratio of quick assets means the quick ratio is calculated in the same way as current ratio but without the less liquid current assets, such as inventory. Inventory might be slowly converted to cash in a business with a long operating cycle. Current liabilities are all the debts that fall due within one year. The ratio reveals the company's ability to pay its short-term debts with cash and receivables. A ratio of less than 1 could suggest difficulty in meeting immediate (quick) commitments. Table 4-2 presents some meaning of the quick ratio levels, which vary by industry.

Table 4-2. Quick ratio.

Quick ratio	Indication of the meaning
>1.0	Excellent
0.7–1.0	Good
0.3–0.6	Passable
<0.3	Weak

The quick ratio measures a company's short-term debt–paying ability. It shows how the company's most liquid (quick) assets cover its current liabilities.

Compared with the current ratio, the quick ratio is a more specific measure of a company's ability to meet its short-term obligations. A ratio of less than 1:1 indicates that a small company is overly dependent on inventory and on future sales to satisfy its short-term debt. A quick ratio of more than 1:1 indicates a good ability to manage short-term liabilities—that is, a greater degree of financial security.

Working Capital

Formula

(Current assets − Current liabilities)

Definition

Working capital is another measure often used to express the relationship between current assets and current liabilities. It shows whether the company is in a sound financial position or is heading for financial difficulties. The amount of working capital that a company needs to remain solvent varies with the size of the organization and the nature of the business activities. The principal factors affecting the quality of working capital are (1) the nature of the current assets and (2) the length of time required to convert these assets to cash.

In evaluating the debt-paying ability of a business, short-term creditors should consider the quality of working capital as well as total monetary value. Negative working capital does not automatically mean that the company is insolvent. A company with adequate working capital should be able to meet its obligations as they mature. A restricted working capital position often causes slowness in trade payments.

The following issues cause changes in working capital:

❑ Sales are increasing and customers are slow in paying their bills. Consequently, accounts receivable increase.

❑ In a large project, projected sales increase and larger inventory volumes must be maintained to finish the project.

Net Working Capital Rotation

Net Sales/Net Working Capital

Formula

$$\frac{\text{Net sales}}{\text{Net working capital}}$$

Net working capital rotation shows how efficiently current assets and current liabilities are used.

Summary

❑ A working capital position that is too restricted can cause trade payment slowness.

Leverage

❑ Leverage ratios show the company's degrees of indebtedness. A highly leveraged condition means a high ratio of debts to equity.

Debt Ratio

Formula

Total liabilities
Total assets

Definition

Debt ratio shows financial leverages compared to the book value of assets and liabilities and shareholders' equity. Book value is the current value of an asset, as shown on the balance sheet.

Common shareholders are pleased to see a high debt ratio, which produces maximum profits in case management is able to earn a rate of return on assets greater than the rate of interest paid to creditors. However, a high debt ratio can be unfavorable if the return on assets falls below the rate of interest paid to creditors, because the borrowed funds are earning less than the interest paid from loans.

Debt ratio indicates to creditors whether a company can pay its debts. If a company is unable to pay its debts, creditors and investors lose their money. The advantage of a high debt ratio is a high interest rate for a company.

Summary

❑ A debt ratio that is too high indicates danger in the company's solvency.

❏ A debt ratio that is too low could indicate the company's unwillingness to invest and grow.

Equity Ratio

Formula

Shareholders' equity
Total assets (average)

Definition

Equity ratio—that is, equity to total assets—shows solvency of the company. It measures the capital structure—that is, owners' funds compared to total assets. The ratio shows a buffer against possible losses. A net loss from the income statement (profit and loss statement) is transferred to decrease the company's own equity on the balance sheet.

The higher the equity in relation to debt, the more stable the financial condition of the company. A company with a highly leveraged condition should be monitored as frequently as possible. In practice, quarterly monitoring is feasible, especially if the company is listed on a stock exchange. Table 4-3 shows some meanings of the equity ratio levels.

Summary

❏ An equity ratio that is too low indicates financial difficulties.

❏ An equity ratio that is too high might indicate an inability to use debt financing.

Table 4-3. Equity ratio.

Equity ratio	Indication of the meaning
>45%	Excellent
36%–45%	Good
21%–35%	Satisfactory
11%–20%	Weak
<10%	Poor

Interest Coverage

Times interest earned measures the coverage of debt.

Formula

$$\frac{\text{Operating income (EBIT)}}{\text{Annual interest expenses}}$$

Definition

Interest coverage is called *times interest earned*. Interest coverage shows financial leverage—that is, how many times interest expenses can be paid by operating income. It shows the extent to which earnings are available to cover interest expenses. If the coverage is poor, a company has difficulties in covering its interests. The higher the ratio, the better.

A high ratio indicates that the company would have little difficulty meeting the interest payments on its loans; creditors of your supplier see this as a sign of safety for future loans.

A low ratio indicates that the company is overextended in its debts; earnings will not be able to cover its debt service if the ratio is less than 1:1. The interest coverage ratio should be higher than 3:1. However, an interest earned ratio of 4:1 to 6:1 is safer, and many creditors look for this in a company as a favorable subject to finance. If the ratio is below 1:1, management is under tremendous pressure to raise cash. The risk of default or bankruptcy is high.

Summary

❏ Interest coverage that is too low might indicate a poor ability to pay contractual interest payments.

Gearing

Formula

$$\frac{\text{(long-term and short-term liabilities} - \text{cash and cash equivalents)}}{\text{Shareholders' equity}}$$

Definition

Gearing expresses the debt-to-equity ratio, which is the relationship between different types of funds in a company, such as loans and equity. The higher the amount of debt, the higher the amount of fixed interest charges in the income statement.

Gearing is 100 percent when a company's debt capital is equal in value to its equity capital. A company is considered to be highly geared when debt exceeds equity in its capital structure. The more highly geared that a company is, the more vulnerable it is to take-overs and bankruptcy.

Net Debt/EBITDA

EBITDA refers to earnings before interest, taxes, depreciation, and amortization.

Formula

$$\frac{\text{(Long-term and short-term liabilities} - \text{cash} - \text{advances paid)}}{\text{(EBIT} + \text{depreciation} + \text{amortization)}}$$

Definition

This ratio shows the ability of EBITDA to cover net debts. If the ratio is high, it takes a long time to pay back the net debt with this EBITDA level. If EBITDA is negative, it does not allow for the repayment of loans.

Summary

❑ Net debt/EBITDA that is too low or negative indicates the company's inability to repay debts with its earnings.

Investment

❑ Market value or investment ratios show investors the value of the company. Evaluate your supplier from the investor's point of view.

Dividend per Share

Formula

$$\text{Dividend per share} = \frac{\text{Dividends announced during the period}}{\text{Number of shares in issue}}$$

Definition

The dividend per share ratio relates the dividends announced during a period to the number of shares in issue during the same period.

Investment ratio provides an indication of the cash return that an investor receives from holding shares in a company.

Earnings per Share

Formula

$$\text{Earnings per share} = \frac{\text{Earnings available to ordinary shareholders}}{\text{Number of ordinary shares in issue}}$$

Definition

The earnings per share (EPS) value of a company relates the earnings generated by the company during a period and available to shareholders to the number of shares in issue.

This ratio is considered to be a fundamental measure of share performance. The trend in EPS over time is used to help assess the investment potential of a company's shares.

Summary

❑ An earnings per share figure that is too low shows an unprofitable investment for the investor.

Key Findings: Steps to Increase Risk

A financially weak company shows poor financial figures in different areas such as efficiency, solvency, and profitability. By analyzing financial statements with ratios, an external audience can anticipate potential problems and identify important strengths in advance. Comparative analysis can show troubles such as:

Low Profitability
Stage 1: Risks are rising as cash flow from operations is decreasing.

1. Decreasing sales and falling profit margins
2. Increasing administrative or R&D costs compared to sales
3. Growing inventories compared to total assets

A declining trend in gross profit margin and operating profit margin is a sign of decreasing profitability. A combination of balance sheet and statement of income–based figures such as ROA, ROE, and weak net sales turnover indicates weak profitability.

Weak Efficiency and Solvency
Stage 2: Risks are increasing when clear signs of insufficient financing appear.

1. Payments to suppliers become slower.
2. Raw material shortages appear.
3. Credit risk increases; bonds are falling to noninvestment grade.

Solvency is a combination of liquidity and leverage. A weak solvency is the result of poor liquidity ratios such as poor current ratio, quick ratio, or low or negative working capital and highly leveraged conditions such as high debt ratio, low equity ratio, or low interest coverage. Weakness shows in liquidity ratios and a highly leveraged condition. As a result of weak solvency, a company has difficulties in payments.

Weak Solvency and Profitability
Stage 3: Risks are high when serious signs of financial difficulties take place.

1. Selling of assets—fixed assets; plant, equipment, and current assets; accounts receivable
2. High indebtedness
3. Fall in credit rating to the lowest grade

Key Questions

The most significant questions are marked with an asterisk.

Growth

❑ Are net sales increasing or decreasing? Why?*
❑ Is the growth of net sales very quick? If so, check the trend of quick ratio and current ratio.*
❑ Does the company have enough funds to support the growth?

Profitability

❑ What is the level of gross margin? If gross margin is low, what is the reason?*
❑ What is the level of gross margin in this industry?

❑ Has gross margin changed? Why?*

❑ What is the level of operating margin?

❑ Has the growth been profitable?

❑ What is the trend of operating profit?*

❑ What is the level of operating margin in this industry?

❑ Is operating margin high enough to cover interest and taxes? If not, what is the company going to do to increase its profitability?

❑ What is the level of ROA?

❑ Has ROA changed? Why?

❑ What is the level of ROE? Is it better than that of other companies in the same industry?

❑ Is this company a profitable investment for its owners?

Efficiency

❑ What is net asset turnover? If the figure is low, the company is using capital ineffectively.

❑ Is the company using its net assets effectively?

❑ How many times does the inventory turn per year? If inventory turnover is slow, it means more funds are needed to finance the inventory.*

❑ Has inventory turnover remained steady or decreased during a period of increased sales? If inventory turnover remains steady and sales increase, the inventory turnover is better and the company is more efficient.

❑ What is the collection period (accounts receivable turnover)? If it is very slow, the company is slow to get trade receivables from its customers.*

❑ Has accounts receivable turnover decreased during a period of increased sales? If so, the company is slow to collect receivables.

❑ What is the average period (how many days) debtors take to pay? If the payable period is long, debtors are financing the business of the company, either willingly or unwillingly.

❑ Is the collection period longer than it has been? Why?*

❑ What is the payable period?*

❑ Is the payable period longer than it has been? Why?*

Liquidity

❑ What is the level of quick ratio?*

❑ What is the level of current ratio? If quick ratio and current ratio are low, it indicates a poor short-term financial position.

❑ What is the interest cover? Can the company afford to pay interest obligations?*

❑ Is there a relationship among the trend and status of the current ratio, quick ratio, accounts receivable, and inventory turnover?

Leverage

❑ What is the debt ratio—that is, debt to assets (or equity ratio, that is, equity to assets)?*

❑ Is indebtedness too high?*

❑ Is the company running into debt too quickly?*

❑ How many years will it take the company to pay back its debts?

❑ If there is a weak cash flow position, is it industry or management related?

❑ If a cash flow problem does exist, is the company using suppliers to finance operations (by paying its suppliers late), or is it seeking additional financing, recapitalization, or investors for an IPO?

❑ What is the possibility of finding external financing?

Key Ratios—Issues for Special Attention

Select key ratios from different groups and compare the trend of key ratios such as growth, profitability, liquidity, efficiency, and leverage analysis.

❑ Make sure that the company has a highly qualified auditor

with a good reputation. The quality of financial statements is essential for providing reliable information.

❑ Compare financial ratios with the company's ratios of previous years along with the ratios of other companies in the same business.

❑ Do not assume that key figures will tell you the entire truth about the company. You must also take into account qualitative factors. (See Chapter 5.)

❑ Do not believe that key figures are exact if the company's accounting practices are too creative. (Remember the Enron case.) Accounting practices and bookkeeping can be creative especially in small companies.

❑ Keep in mind that ratios cannot be better than the original figures in financial statements.

❑ Do not assume that a supplier with high debts and poor profitability can make all the necessary investments.

4.6 Forecasting

A forecast is an extension of historical patterns and relationships based on future assumptions, such as a company's technological success, competition, management decisions, and future economic condition. Even with the best assumptions, it is impossible to predict in great detail what future financial statements will look like. Any projected financial information is only as good as the underlying information and assumptions. If the information is misleading, the assumptions based on it will inherit the same weaknesses.

A significant difference between the actual and forecast results might show management's inability to make accurate forecasts. If the company has made misleading assumptions before, would it be able to make better forecasts now? It is important to check the source of the differences, such as (1) customers (lower or higher sales than expected) or loss of a customer; (2) suppliers, difficulties with suppliers, higher or lower purchasing prices; or (3) industry trend, better or worse industry trend than expected.

The quality of the financial statements and the company's forecast is essential. If you can get internal information directly from the company, it can help you to make accurate forecasts. You can take the company's own forecast and analyze it to see whether it overestimates the company's profitability and sources of funds in the future. There are several sophisticated methods to use for forecasting the future. It is essential to evaluate the possible gap between the source and use of funds and the possibilities to get financing—that is, to raise equity financing or increase liabilities.

The best possible guess about the future is based on historical facts. It is possible to make an analysis, such as a sensitivity analysis and trend simulation. A sensitivity analysis is a simple method of analysis. It is based on questions about possible outcomes: What if net sales are lower than expected? What if administrative costs are higher than expected? A sensitivity analysis provides a good foundation for estimating the company's future, because it can take into account possible risks, find alternative ways to avoid troubles, and assess the assumptions the estimates are based on.

Computer-based trend simulation programs extend the scope and speed of analysis. The programs provide a quick method for changing assumptions and receiving new outcomes. The disadvantage is that you may limit your scope to only the computer-based results and forget the qualitative facts that do not appear in the computer program.

The statements of income, balance sheet, and cash flow statement from the two previous years should be available. It is preferable to have financial statements for three or more years to determine the business trend. If the company is in a stable industry sector, its past financial statements reflect the future financial situation better than if the company were in an unstable and/or growing industry.

If the company is a start-up business, the traditional forecast methods based on the previous financial statements have little use in financial projection. It is much more demanding to make a forecast for a start-up business or a fast-growing business than for an existing and relatively stable business. Historical financial statements are normally available from existing companies. It is relatively easy to see trends. Underlying assumptions such as the company's market share, products, services, and ownership play a more significant role in forecasting when assessing a start-up company or fast-growing company. Both of these characteristics—start-up and fast growing—were predominant in the telecommunications operator business in 2000 and 2001.

Tips for Forecasting

Items helpful in analyzing forecasts and their effects include:

Items	Tips
Lower sales than expected	❑ The effect on profitability. Does the change convert a net income to a net loss?
Higher costs than expected	❑ Due to net loss, shareholders' equity decreases on the balance sheet.
	❑ Due to the decreased shareholders' equity (lower equity ratio, higher debt-to-equity, more leveraged company), there will be a need to increase shareholders' equity. Are the current owners willing to increase their investment in the company or possibly pursue new owners?
	❑ Personnel, administrative, and material costs are higher than expected, so operating profit will be lower than expected.
	❑ Other costs, such as restructuring costs, are expected. If a company is closing several factories, there will be restructuring costs.

There should be no differences between sources and uses of funds. Significant differences between the expected sources and uses of funds should trigger an evaluation of whether those differences are indicative of possible financial difficulties.

It is essential to remember that onetime gains and onetime charges affect net income. These adjustments include, for example, (1) gains and losses from selling or discontinuing a line of business, or (2) changes in net income resulting from changes in accounting methods.

The key questions that follow can help you to better forecast your supplier's business. You do not necessarily need to answer all the questions. The questions provide guidelines for your analysis.

Key Questions

The most significant questions are marked with an asterisk.

Future

❑ What are the future plans of the company?*

❑ Is management highlighting the company's plans clearly or is it giving only vague, general comments?

Sales

❑ What are the projected sales for the next two or three years?*

❑ Can the company grow faster than the industry average? If so, how or why?*

Cost of Goods Sold

❑ What is the best estimation of changes in material costs, labor costs, etc.?*

❑ If sales will be lower than in previous years, how flexible is the company's cost structure (fixed costs, variable costs)?

Other Costs

❑ How will R&D costs be allocated?*

❑ What is the percentage of annual R&D costs?*

❑ Will there be acquisition costs or gains from discontinued operations?

❑ How is depreciation allocated? Is the company going to lengthen or shorten the write-off period? Why?

Interest Expense

❑ What is the current amount of interest-bearing debt financing?*

❑ What is the assumable interest level?*

Taxes

❑ What is the statutory tax rate?

Cash Flow

❑ How much profit does the company expect to generate in the future?

❑ How will the working capital change? *Note:* Cash and borrowing will affect this item.

❑ Is the company going to invest heavily in fixed assets, such as plant and equipment?

❑ Is the company going to make any acquisitions?

❑ Does the company customarily pay dividends? What has been the rate of dividends?

❑ What will be the repayment of current maturities of long-term debt?

❑ Is the company going to increase debt financing?

Assumptions

❑ What information is the forecast based on?

❑ What are the assumptions?*

❑ Have you tested the assumptions in a sensitivity analysis?* Assumptions might include market growth or investor willingness to invest in the company.

❑ Is the company going to introduce profitable new products in the future?

❑ Does the company represent future technology?

Political and Regulatory Requirements

❑ What are the current and anticipated political situations in the country?*

❑ Does the political situation have any effect on the company?

❑ Will the regulatory environment change?

❑ How will a new regulatory environment affect the company?

Market

❑ What is the expected growth in this industry?

❑ How is the market expected to change?*

❑ Is an overall depression expected?

During high periods, most companies perform well on the market. By contrast, during a recession, nearly all companies have difficulties on the market.

❑ Is competition going to increase?

Financing

- ❑ How will the company finance its future investments?*
- ❑ In general, is the market for public offerings good in this industrial sector?
- ❑ Are banks willing to increase debt financing to the company?
- ❑ Is the investment going to be financed by long-term or short-term loans?
- ❑ If the company prefers short-term financing, how can it amortize the loans?
- ❑ How much lower will profitability be allowed to drop?
- ❑ What are the minimum requirements of profitability to allow for the repayment of loans?

Forecasting—Issues for Special Attention

To track cash flow generation, the following items must be monitored:

- ❑ Monitor your forecast and make corrections when you receive updated information on the company and the market.
- ❑ Take into account all information available, not only the previous financial statements.
- ❑ Keep in mind that your forecast cannot be better than the underlying material (assumptions) used for the forecast.
- ❑ Remember that the projection for a start-up company is more demanding to execute. A special challenge arose during the economic slowdown. Companies established during an economic slowdown are normally more vulnerable than companies with long-established customer, supplier, and financier relationships.
- ❑ Try to uncover the "real" truth through your forecast. You can assume that your forecast as a company outsider is less accurate than the company's own forecast. If it is not, then you should be hired by the company to project its future.

4.7 Differences Between U.S. GAAP and IFRS Accounting Standards

This subchapter compares the differences between two well-known and commonly used accounting standards: the U.S. Generally Accepted Accounting Rules (GAAP) and International Accounting Standards (IAS), now known as International Financial Reporting Standards (IFRS). The comparison is made of the items most relevant in analyzing suppliers. If you are interested in studying the differences between accounting standards more thoroughly, some of the publications in the bibliography may be helpful, in particular *Comparative International Accounting,* by Christopher Nobes and Robert Parker (1995); and "GAAP Differences in Your Pocket: IAS and US GAAP," by Deloitte Touche Tohmatsu (July 2002, www.iasplus.com).

Companies and investors are forced to look for new markets in the global environment to extend their businesses. New business partners want to assess their foreign customers or suppliers. The need for international accounting standards is clear because of the globalization of capital markets. As business and trade barriers between nations become less restrictive, differences among national accounting standards become more troubling. Therefore, accounting standards should be similar to enable comparisons among companies. Investors are willing to invest their money in the most globally profitable companies. A major step in standardization will occur in 2005 when all publicly listed companies, with few exceptions, will be required to prepare their consolidated financial statements in accordance with IFRS.

The Major Differences in Accounting Standards

Figure 4-12 summarizes some of the differences between IFRS and U.S. GAAP. Only the differences that primarily affect the analysis of suppliers have been selected. The following are only guidelines and might vary according to industry and the nature of the company's operations.

Reasons for Differences in Accounting Standards

The differences in accounting standards and principles affect financial reporting practices and the information presented in financial statements. For a quantitative analysis based on financial statements, it is important to consider the difference in accounting practices when commenting on the international comparison of financial ratios. The major differences in accounting practices in each country are based

Figure 4-12. Selected comparison of IFRS and U.S. GAAP.

Topic	IFRS	U.S. GAAP
General approach	Principle-based standards with limited application guidance.	Rule-based standards with more specific application guidance.
Ability to make choices	Generally more choices.	Generally fewer choices.
Financial statement presentation	Specific line items required.	Certain standards require specific presentation of certain items. Public companies are subject to SEC rules and regulations, which require specific line items.
Departure from a standard when compliance would be misleading	Permitted in "extremely rare" circumstances "to achieve a fair presentation."	Not directly addressed in U.S. GAAP literature, although an auditor may conclude that by applying a certain GAAP requirement the financial statements are misleading, thereby allowing for an "override."
Reversal of inventory write-downs	Required, if certain criteria are met.	Prohibited.
Basis of inventory	Carried at the lower of cost and net realizable value (NRV).	Carried at the lower of cost and market (market is the lower of replacement cost and NRV minus normal profit margin).
Correction of errors	May either restate prior financial statements or include the cumulative effect in net profit and loss in the current financial statements.	Must restate prior financial statements.
Basis of reportable segments	Lines of business and geographical areas.	Components for which information is reported internally to top management, which may or may not be based on lines of business or geographical areas.
Types of segment disclosures	Required disclosures for both "primary" and "secondary" segments.	Only one basis of segmentation, although certain "enterprisewide" disclosures are required such as revenue from major customers and revenue by country.
Accounting basis for reportable segments	Amounts are based on IFRS GAAP measures.	Amounts are based on whatever basis is used for internal reporting purposes.
Basis of property, plant, and equipment	May use either fair value or historical cost.	Generally required to use historical cost.
Purchased in-process R&D	Capitalize and amortize over the estimated useful life, which is presumed to be twenty years or less.	Expense.
Goodwill	Must capitalize and amortize goodwill over its estimated useful life, which is presumed to be twenty years or less, subject to an impairment test.	Must capitalize, but not amortize, subject to an impairment test.
Negative goodwill	Initially offset against any expected future losses, then amortize any amounts not exceeding the value of acquired nonmonetary assets; any excess is included in net profit or loss.	Initially allocate on a pro rata basis against the carrying amounts of certain acquired nonfinancial assets, with any excess recognized as an extraordinary gain.

(continues)

Figure 4-12. (continued)

Topic	IFRS	U.S. GAAP
Basis of consolidation policy	Control (look to governance and risk and benefits).	Majority voting rights.
Development costs	Capitalize, if certain criteria are met.	Expense.
Purchased intangibles (other than in process R&D)	Capitalize and amortize over the estimated useful life, which is presumed to be twenty years or less.	Capitalize. Amortize if the asset has a finite life. Do not amortize if the asset has an indefinite life, but test regularly for impairment.

Source: Deloitte Touche Tohmatsu, "GAAP Differences in Your Pocket: IAS and US GAAP" © 2002.

on differences in, for example, the legal system, taxation rules, and ownership and financing of a company.

Law

The legal system of each country has a strong bearing on the style of accounting standards adopted. The distinctive differences in legal systems follow two main approaches—Roman and common law:

1. *Roman law, code law, or Napoleonic law* provides detailed rules and regulations in codes or statutes as the main source of law. This implies a great deal of central control in all activities. The following countries follow Roman law: France, Germany, Italy, the Netherlands, Spain, Portugal, Belgium, Switzerland, and Japan.

2. *Common law and equity law* is developed based on precedent or new interpretations of the basic law. This is a more laissez-faire approach where accepted rules are built up over time. Common law is valid in the United Kingdom, Ireland, Austria, New Zealand, Hong Kong, Singapore, and Canada.

Taxation

One of the driving forces has been taxation of the country. Taxation rules provide guidelines on what constitutes taxable income.

Ownership and Financing

Financial statements hold different meanings and have different uses in how companies acquire financing. As a simultaneous owner and financier, a bank has more comprehensive knowledge of the company's financial statements than an investor, who buys stock via the stock exchange. The most significant difference between privately and publicly owned companies is the requirement to prepare and publish financial statements. The requirements for preparing financial statements are more detailed for publicly owned companies than for privately owned companies.

A Practical Guide to Accounting Differences

This section presents the differences in the basic requirements in privately and publicly owned companies in selected countries. The discussion is limited to ownership and the extent to publish financial accounts. It is impossible to conduct a reliable quantitative analysis of a supplier without obtaining comprehensive financial statements from the company. The following text provides some basic guidelines for obtaining financial information in selected countries. As stated previously, an analysis is only as good as the fundamental information on which it is based.

United States

In the United States, the Financial Accounting Standards Board (FASB) is responsible for developing U.S. GAAP. The FASB is the authority for establishing accounting standards in the United States. Publicly listed companies need to file reports in compliance with the requirements of the Securities and Exchange Commission (SEC).

Ownership

The United States characteristically has widespread ownership of shares in public companies, mainly by institutional investors. Therefore, the requirements of investors and the stock exchange have been the main influences on published accounts and have produced a much greater level of discipline. However, the discipline has not been strict enough, allowing cases like Enron to occur.

Standards in the United States are relatively strict and more complex than those in other countries. The quoted companies in the United States must deliver several forms, including the so-called SEC filings, 10-K, 10-Q, and quarterly reports, which consist of an income statement, balance sheet, and cash flow statement.

The international companies listed on the New York Stock Exchange (NYSE) are required to submit financial statements that adhere to GAAP, which can reflect significant differences compared with the statements prepared in the company's home country. A company reporting a profit based on the accounting standards in its own country may report a loss in GAAP. (*Note:* SEC filings are discussed in more detail in the Appendix under App. 6 Company Information.)

There is little information available from privately owned U.S.-based companies. The companies can disclose the financial information to outsiders if they feel it is important for their business. If their customer is important, they might disclose some financial figures and information on their current status and possibly about their future plans. Generally, this information is possible to obtain in face-to-face contacts.

United Kingdom Ownership

In the United Kingdom, as in the United States, widespread ownership of shares in public companies is a characteristic feature. The companies are owned mostly by institutional investors.

As stated earlier, it is relatively difficult to obtain information from privately owned companies. In the United Kingdom, privately owned companies send their files to the Companies House, where the files are publicly available.

Japan Ownership

Publicly listed companies in Japan mainly belong to different larger groups, called *keiretsu*. The companies in a *keiretsu* make up a company group in which the companies are owned by each other. There is often a bank within the *keiretsu*. The requirements for published financial information have been limited because of the ownership. The main owners have direct contact with the board of directors and typically have a representative on it. Until recently, publicly owned companies in Japan needed to deliver an income statement and balance sheet only once a year unless something unexpected had occurred to affect the company's performance—for example, a poor investment that generated significant losses. The practice has changed and companies now must deliver financial information semi-annually. The needs of external parties, such as investors and customers, have prompted Japanese companies to start creating informative annual reports in English.

Privately held companies in Japan almost always have their financial statements in Japanese only. If there is an English version, it has been shortened and does not necessarily include all the important details.

Germany Ownership

In Germany, the stock market is relatively small, so there are relatively few publicly listed companies. Banks, insurance companies, and large shareholders own many companies. The largest owners have directors on the board and therefore have access to as much information as they need.

In Germany, Austria, and Switzerland, there is only a limited amount of financial information available from public sources, for example, from credit reports like a Dun & Bradstreet report. The information mostly reflects reported sales, fixed assets, receivables, and short-term loans. But even with those figures, it is not possible to calculate the current ratio or equity ratio to gain better insight as to the financial position of the company. Privately owned companies deliver their financial accounts to a trade registry (chamber of commerce) in the company's hometown. This information is open to public inspection. Accounts must also be published in the *Federal Gazette* (*Bundesanzeiger*).

Case 3: Visit to a Japanese Company Highlights Cultural Differences

Jill took her first business trip to Japan with an audit group of four experienced employees who had conducted business in Japan several times. Jill's knowledge about Japan and the Japanese people was limited. She was a friend of a Japanese-American couple; the wife was American and her husband Japanese. Diane had told her about the challenges women faced in the Japanese business world.

In Tokyo

The other members of Jill's group were already waiting in the lobby; all of them were wearing dark suits and ties. They were expected to meet the president of the company and key people of various functions. Their visit was well prepared, thanks to the audit team's leader, the head auditor Pekka Tila.

The company they visited was called JapanX Ltd. The driver for JapanX was waiting for them outside with a large green car. A man with short hair parted on the side, who was wearing a white cutter shirt and a dark blue suit, approached them, smiling and bowing slightly, "Konnichiwa, good morning." Pekka Tila's audit group bowed slightly and answered politely, "Konnichiwa." Pekka Tila continued, "Nice to see you, Shiraishi-san." Masanobu Shiraishi was their contact person—a salesperson at JapanX Ltd.

After a thirty-minute drive, they arrived at JapanX Ltd. When Jill saw the company's sign, a strange feeling overcame her. How would she manage? Jill looked at the men sitting next to her with their dark suits. They had been to Japanese companies many times. The car door opened automatically. Two Japanese men were standing outside, smiling and bowing.

"Nice to meet you, please come in." The men escorted the guests into the building. To Jill, it felt like hours had passed before the elevator stopped. The door opened and she stepped out with the men. On the left were four young women who were wearing white blouses, dark blue vests, and dark blue skirts. They were sitting and giggling. Jill realized that they must be the "office ladies" (a term used in Japan to distinguish women office workers in nonmanagement positions). She smiled at them. Maybe it was unexpected, because they looked slightly embarrassed and giggled more, bowing their heads.

The group was guided to a large room that contained a long table. At one end, there was a screen and a projector, and at the other end, nice, comfortable sofas. The audit group was seated facing the door. Jill took two steps back as she waited to see where the men from her company would sit. Jill hoped that they knew the rules. The purchasing manager from the Japanese office of Success Inc. was seated nearest to the projector. Pekka was going to give a presentation; he sat next to Mr. Okazaki, the purchasing manager of Success Inc. Jill found herself sitting at the middle of the long table.

The audit group stood up when the lineup of hosts entered. Everyone shook hands, bowed, and presented their business cards. Jill looked desperate because she was running low on business cards. "I'm Takanobu Suzuki, pleased to meet you," a gray-haired man said in a Japanese accent as he bowed to Jill. "Pleased to meet you, Mr. Suzuki," Jill replied, trying to remember all their names. "I'm Jill Turner." Jill bowed politely and took his business card. Jill placed all the cards face up on the table.

A glance at Jill's colleague Steven Smith showed that she needed to arrange the cards in a neat row. Jill had to keep track of the most important persons. Jill leaned over slightly to Eric and whispered, "Which one is Mr. Suzuki, the president?" He quietly answered, "The gentleman directly in front of you."

For a brief moment, Jill was shocked. Her face may have turned red, but she tried to remain calm. She realized that they had taken the wrong seats. Jill's books had told her that the most important persons should sit opposite each other. Pekka should sit in her seat and she in Pekka's seat. Pekka chose the seat in the front because it was the nearest place to give a presentation. He was correct in his thinking—if they were in Europe—but now they were in Japan.

Pekka started his presentation of Success Inc.: their goals, a brief overview of the business plan, and sourcing strategy. He gave a fluent presentation. His illustrations were clear. He spoke English clearly and slowly. It was easy to follow him as he went from one figure to the next.

Jill glanced at Mr. Suzuki, who was ahead of her. He was in his sixties and had gray hair. His eyes were almost closed, and he nodded off. Jill looked at the annual report they had been given. On the second page of the annual report, the same man was smiling proudly. Jill looked at the picture in the annual report and at Mr. Suzuki ahead of her. The same person. The picture was new.

His section in the annual report said, "The last year was a year of restructuring." His first words on the page. "What was the result?" Jill wondered. "It must not have been very good with words like that." Jill turned the pages until she reached the section on financial highlights. The operating profit was 4,000 million yen, net loss 10,000 million yen. The previous years had shown a profit. What caused the loss in the last year? Jill wondered as she listened to Pekka's speech.

Vice president of marketing Mr. Satoka started his presentation on JapanX Ltd. "We have been in the market for over forty years. Our company is listed on the Tokyo and Osaka stock exchanges. We have a good reputation in the market. For over thirty years we have cooperated with well-known Japanese companies." Mr. Satoka's English was fluent, with a slight Japanese accent. Jill followed his presentation by trying to figure out the reason behind the loss. No direct mention was made of it, and he finished his speech.

Two office ladies came in to serve coffee. One of them wore a mask over her mouth. It looked strange. Jill leaned over to Kalle. "Why is she covering her mouth." He replied, "She probably has the flu, and in Japan it is not allowable to infect other people."

They were served coffee and Japanese cookies. The Japanese men did not acknowledge the presence of the women. It seemed to be time for discussion. Jill faced the men, with the president across from her. "I believe there was some famous artist who said that we have to live life as well as we can," he said and looked her. Jill offered her best smile and answered, "That is very interesting. Very clever ideas. It is useful to read books. I have always liked them." "Yes, the ideas are very deep. I think that we have a lot to learn." His English was not very good, and Jill had some difficulty following his speech.

Jill smiled again and they engaged in casual small talk. The others listened, and after a while, they joined in on the polite discussion. Mr. Takaoke turned the discussion back to business and proposed that the audit group go to the groups according to the agenda.

Jill was expected to go alone to see five men from the finance department. Jill sent her questions beforehand and the representatives of JapanX had prepared answers for her. Jill was relieved to have the list of questions, because it would help to prevent the gaps in the conversation. Especially in Japan, people like to be well prepared; they want to obtain an agenda well in advance—particularly if they do not know the person well.

Jill followed the men to the other room. "Hello, my name is Mr. Takaschi," one man said, shaking her hand. He spoke English fluently. "I have studied and worked in the United States for three years. I am translating for our vice president of finance, Mr. Cita." Mr. Cita looked at Jill, nodded, and said, "We apologize if we haven't understood all your questions correctly. Please let us know and we'll try to do our best." All five men looked at her and nodded slightly.

"Shall we start now with question number one?" Mr. Takaschi asked, reading Jill's questions. "Yes, please, let's go through the questions on the list and I may have some additional questions after I hear your answers." The men looked at each other but did not say anything.

They proceeded question by question. Mr. Takaschi translated and the other men spoke in Japanese with each other. Jill sat quietly and waited until they had finished their internal explanations.

"Your sales decreased 20 percent from the previous year and profit was lower than before. Was there any special reason for that?" Jill looked at the consolidated statements of income and turned to the men. All were quiet. The vice president of finance, Mr. Cita, smiled but did not want to respond to the question. Then he said something in Japanese to his subordinates. Mr. Takaschi turned to Jill, "The market for our main product semiconductors went down last year. We didn't react to the new situation quickly enough. Now we are recovering from the situation. In the last quarter we showed a slight profit."

Mr. Cita looked down and the situation was slightly unpleasant. The room was quiet. Mr. Takaschi looked at Jill steadily, implying that this question had been handled. A normal, realistic explanation she thought, turning to the next point, the low equity ratio, which was only 8 percent.

The main owners were Japanese banks and insurance companies. This company might not go bankrupt, but it might not be able to invest in the required new machinery because the company had a low shareholders' equity ratio and high liabilities.

"Your equity ratio is low," Jill said and looked at Mr. Takaschi. They sat quietly. Mr. Cita answered momentarily. Then Mr. Takaschi told Jill that the low equity ratio was hardly a problem. "Our owners support us. We have had the same owners all along and we have an excellent relationship with them." "How about possible investments?" Jill asked. Again, Mr. Takaschi translated and the brief answer came: "We will make all the needed investments."

Mr. Takaschi turned to Jill, "Mr. Cita is unfortunately very busy. Do you have any more questions?" Jill looked at the list of questions and stated that she could continue with the other men. Jill had barely finished her sentence when Mr. Cita quickly stood up. He bowed slightly and left the room.

"Was that your last question?" Mr. Takaschi asked as the other men studied Jill carefully. The accounting manager, Mr. Takanobu, smiled and gave a small gift to Jill. The men said something in Japanese and then Mr. Takaschi said to Jill: "Here is a small gift for you. We hope you will enjoy it." Jill opened the nicely wrapped present. "There are two books: One is of Japanese customs and the other is the only book we were able to find explaining Japanese accounting rules in English," Mr. Takaschi explained proudly. The books had brown and gray covers without any pictures. Jill politely thanked the men for the books. This was a welcome gift.

The audit team gave a positive audit report and corporate analysis of JapanX Ltd.

Success Inc. and JapanX Ltd. established close cooperation to develop the quality of their products. Both companies benefited from the profitable cooperation. Jill had follow-up meetings with JapanX. The Japanese company developed its accounting systems and produced more timely internal reports than it did previously. The main owner supported JapanX financially. JapanX also became profitable because of the improvements in its quality and products.

Key Points

Corporate Analysis

Corporate analysis is a comprehensive analysis that creates a picture of your supplier's capability as a company. It answers the question: Is your supplier a solvent and profitable company that will remain in business?

Corporate analysis consists of quantitative and qualitative analysis of the company. Quantitative factors come from financial statements such as the balance sheet, statement of income, cash flow statement, and calculated key figures based on financial statements. Forecasting extends the scope of analysis by allowing the opportunity to consider the future. Quantitative analysis is discussed in Subchapter 4.4.

Qualitative analysis is based on the internal and external factors affecting the company, such as elements in the company's environment and within the company. When evaluating suppliers, it is essential to take into account the qualitative factors, such as the suppliers' other customers, suppliers, market, ownership, and management. Chapter 5 focuses on qualitative analysis, which is based on information provided directly by suppliers and on outside information sources, which are addressed in the Appendix.

Balance Sheet

The balance sheet is a mirror of the past. It shows the financial position of the company at that specific moment. The balance sheet raises the question of "true" value of the assets and the meaning of goodwill. There are weaknesses in the historical cost account. However, the balance sheet is an important document, which, together with statements of income and the cash flow statement, reflects the financial position of the company.

Statement of Income

The statement of income shows the bottom line, or the amount that is left after all costs. If the company is not generating profit, it will not survive for long. Profitability is essential for the company's future. Profit increases shareholders' equity.

Cash Flow Statement

The cash flow statement includes both cash receipts and cash payments from operating activities. In addition, the statement provides information about all investing and financing activities of the company during a specific period of time. The cash flow statement is a practical tool for evaluating the solvency of a business. Solvency is the combination of liquidity and efficiency.

Key Ratios

❏ Make the company measurable.
❏ Show the historical financial performance and trends.
❏ Indicate risks.
❏ Give warning signs.

The trend of the key figures increases the value of the analysis.

Forecasting

Forecast is the best projection you can make without having access to all the facts of the company's financial management. Analytical tools are preferable in forecasting to enable changes in forecasts and quicker results. Forecasting gives you an idea about the future; but you must make the decisions based on these and other facts. Are you going to continue with this supplier or are you going to find a new supplier?

Different Accounting Standards: IFRS and U.S. GAAP

Different legal systems and taxation are the two main reasons for the different accounting systems. The differences between IFRS and U.S. GAAP, which mostly affect the analyses of suppliers, are presented in Subchapter 4.7.

5

Analyzing Qualitative Factors

FINANCIAL STATEMENTS and key ratios should be reviewed together with other factors affecting the company. Financial statement analysis is a quantitative, easily measurable analysis. The analysis is called *qualitative* when other aspects of the company are also analyzed. Qualitative analysis consists of all nonfinancial aspects, which provide a background for the financial profile. Special skills are needed to find relevant nonfinancial aspects and combine them with qualitative facts.

Analyzing suppliers is not simply a matter of filling in boxes and calculating a company's financial ratios; it also involves asking questions, such as those presented in the Key Questions sections. Answers in one area raise more questions and new views of investigation in other areas. There is no common framework that can be applied in exactly the same manner each time.

In qualitative analysis, components such as management, product portfolio, and company structure are assessed and investigated. Parts B and C of the corporate analysis are discussed more closely in this chapter. (See Figure 5-1.)

Financial statements with key ratios were analyzed in Chapter 4. Financial figures are the mirror of the past. The operations of the company affect the financial figures and vice versa. These two issues are closely linked. Reasonable financial figures enable the company to operate. If the company is financially strong, it is better positioned to operate, whereas if the company is financially weak, its manage-

Figure 5-1. Components of corporate analysis of suppliers.

A	EXECUTIVE SUMMARY
	Recommendations Strengths, Weaknesses, Opportunities, and Threats (SWOT) Conclusions Risk rating

B	ENVIRONMENT
	Country Political environment Regulatory environment
	Market Customers Suppliers and logistics Competitors

C	COMPANY
	Strategy Company life cycle Technology Ownership Corporate structure 　　—Holding company 　　—Subsidiary Organization Management Acquisitions and mergers

D	FINANCIAL ANALYSIS

ment must spend more time solving financial problems so the company has fewer opportunities to concentrate on its key business.

After building the skeleton of the quantitative analysis, the next step is akin to adding the muscles of the company. The key relationships of a company are presented in Figure 5-2.

5.1 Environment

A company cannot escape its environment. Environmental factors include customers, competitors, and suppliers. The success of a company is especially dependent on its customers and also its suppliers.

Figure 5-2. Key relationships.

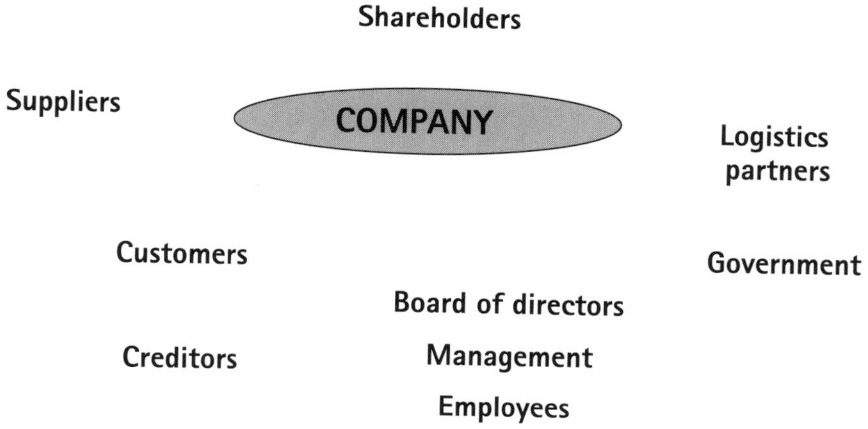

Shareholders

Suppliers

COMPANY

Logistics
partners

Customers

Government

Board of directors

Creditors

Management

Employees

Normally, a company faces competition when there are no restrictions on competition. Each industry also has its own characteristic features, and the average financial key figures vary slightly from industry to industry.

Country

In the country section political and regulatory environment are discussed. Political risks arise from the rules and regulations the government implements. Political risks can exist at both macro- and microlevels. Examples of macrolevel political risks include political change, revolution, or the adoption of new policies by a government, subjecting all companies in the country to political risk. A microlevel political risk, on the other hand, refers to a case in which an individual company, a specific industry, or companies from a particular country are subjected to a takeover.

The regulatory environment involves the establishment of a company's possibilities to do business under current laws and requirements. Changes in the regulatory environment can have a significant positive or negative impact on a company's business.

Market

The line of business affects a company's environment as does the trend in the line of business. Sensitivity to the trend and special features in the field are facts that must be taken into account.

Customers

If customers are not willing to buy a company's products, the company won't last long in the market. A company with several stable and strong customers has better possibilities of avoiding financial difficulties than a company with only a few customers. If a company has only a few financially weak customers, the risk of bad debt increases. A strong and well-known customer base provides stability. Marketing strategy and the basis of the marketing strategy are also important to evaluate.

Suppliers and Logistics

A company faces fewer problems in its deliveries if it has a strong supplier base. The supplier-delivery chain is more flexible. The possibility of difficulties in deliveries increases when the key suppliers are unstable companies. You should ensure that your subsuppliers are performing well, especially if your supplier is manufacturing your products. You can audit and evaluate the processes of your supplier and request that your supplier also audits its suppliers.

Competitors

In new industries, competition is more fragmented. Most companies are new or newly established. Later, the clear market leaders, the medium- and low-level competitors typically emerge. The wave of acquisitions and mergers starts as competition becomes increasingly tougher. A company will have global and local competitors. The analysis of key competitors should include an evaluation of their products, customers, and service concept.

Key Questions

The most significant questions are marked with an asterisk.

Country

❑ What is the current political situation in the supplier's country?

❑ Is the political environment stable?*

❑ Do regulations in this business change frequently?

❑ What are the government policies on taxes and duties?

❑ Can a change in regulations create an unfavorable business climate for the company?

❑ Does the country have currency control?

Market

❑ What is the market position of the company?*

❑ Is the company presenting a top brand?

❑ What is the overall market potential for the product or service?*

Customers

❑ Who are the main customers?*

❑ Are the main customers large or small companies?

❑ What is the percentage of sales to each customer?*

Suppliers and Logistics

❑ Who are the main suppliers of each material?

❑ What is the key supplier's share in purchasing volume?*

❑ Who takes care of the inventory?*

❑ Who arranges the deliveries to the end customers?

Competitors

❑ Who are the main competitors?*

❑ How large are the competitors?*

❑ What is the average quality of the competitors' products and services?

❑ Do the competitors have products that are similar to those of the company?

❑ What has been the pricing policy of the organization: price leader or price follower?

❑ Does the company have any patents? (Check the patents with the patent authorities.)

5.2 Company

This section is a key element in the qualitative analysis. The most important element in ensuring the company's future is strategy that shows the direction in which the company intends to go. The company can be newly established or have a long history, but a clever strategy provides the essential factors to success. However, the length of the company's history matters when evaluating a company. It is important to understand a company's life cycle in order to be able to evaluate the decisions that the company makes. A start-up company faces different challenges from those of an existing company in a mature market.

A company can keep its position in the positive phases of the life cycle if it is able to adopt new technologies. A chosen technology can extend or restrict a company's future possibilities. A company with a great history but with old technologies can be at the end of its life cycle.

Ownership creates the framework for financing. A publicly owned company has better access to external funding than a privately owned company. On the other hand, privately owned small- or medium-size companies have the advantage of quick and flexible decision making.

Corporate structure is discussed in order to find out if there are potential risks somewhere else in the company group other than in the specific part of the company in focus. Understanding the company's structure can reveal completely new issues regarding the company's financial performance. One of the most significant factors of a company's performance is its management. A skillful management creates success for a company, while an inexperienced management can destroy a flourishing business.

Strategy

Strategy has carried slightly different meanings over the course of time. The term *strategy* has been used in wars, in plotting a way to defeat the enemy. Strategy is the key element in victory and success. Strategy is a key element in the company's existence. Why is the company in the market and how will it survive there?

Levels of Strategy

Strategies are defined on different levels. The level of the strategy is specified based on the usage of the strategy. There are three levels of strategy based on organizational structure: corporate, business, and operational or functional.

Corporate strategy is the top-level strategy that asks, "What business or businesses should we be in?" The outcome of the answer determines the structure of a company. The need to change the structure of a company is related to the market situation. Existing and anticipated markets set the guidelines for the strategy. In growing markets, a company normally chooses a growth strategy: horizontal, combining two or more similar types of businesses; or vertical, combining some other part of the supplier chain to the company. In declining markets, asset selling and restructuring are the dominant strategies for surviving in the market. Corporate strategy is set by corporate headquarters.

Business strategy is set at the individual business unit or division level. A larger organization generally has several business units or divisions. The business strategy is the specific strategy to tackle the competition. It is the competitive strategy of the unit. The business strategy explores the ways to compete in this specific business: "How can we compete in this business segment?"

Operational or functional strategy includes the strategies guiding the different organizational functions in their tasks, for example, marketing, production, quality, finance, purchasing, and R&D. Operational strategy asks the question: "How can this function best serve its internal customers?" Operational strategies are set at the functional level and guide the daily activities of the function.

Key Questions

The most significant questions are marked with an asterisk.

History

❑ Does the company have a long history?*
❑ Does the company have a stable history?

Strategy

❑ What is the main strategy?*
❑ Is the company willing to expand its scope to new business areas?*

❑ Is the company too conservative?

❑ Is the company expanding too quickly to business areas out of its scope?*

❑ Is the company willing to grow its business?

❑ Is the chosen business field still growing?

Company Life Cycle

Market is not the only factor defining a strategy. Life cycle also affects the decision on which strategy to choose. Unlike humans, business enterprises experience identical life cycles. In the different life cycle phases, the needs and contributions of the company are different. Understanding the company life cycle is important to give a fair assessment of the company.

There are typical features in every phase of a company's life cycle: start-up, growth, maturity, and declining phases. Particularly from a financial point of view, sales and profitability play significant roles in the different phases. (See Figure 5-3.)

Start-Up Companies

The start-up stage in the business life cycle clearly presents the highest level of business risk. If your supplier is a start-up company, you

Figure 5-3. Company life cycle.

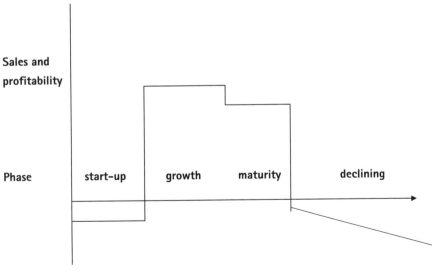

need to check its background and assess the company's risk potential. Start-up companies are mainly funded by their own funds. The owners of a start-up company are essential sources of funding. Risk is associated with several elements of the company, such as products, markets, management, and financing. Start-up companies generally tend to generate losses and they usually have negative cash flow. Which company will succeed and which will eventually lose is the question to which everyone would like to know the answer. Investors and investment analysts try to find the answer to that critical question. The start-up phase is essentially the survival of a company. It is a phase of creating, developing, and getting the idea to the marketplace.

A start-up company has these characteristic features:

❑ High R&D and marketing costs compared to its business volume.

❑ Often generates losses and requires outside financing from investors and bankers.

❑ A short history. It is impossible to evaluate start-ups based on their historical financial figures and to examine trends by using key ratios. Instead, the analysis must include other issues such as evaluation of the business plan and forecasting.

A new company incurs significant costs. It must have enough capital to cover all its start-up costs, such as the lease or purchase of a building and equipment, tools and supplies, advertising, licenses, utilities, and other expenses. Owners should maintain a capital reserve to support the company until it begins to make a profit. It is important in the analysis to find out whether the entrepreneur is overly optimistic in the financial plan and fails to recognize that expenses initially exceed income for most small companies. You can relate your concerns to your supplier, especially if the company is an important supplier for you. In particular, it is risky if the supplier plans to have high sales growth over the next couple of years. This growth may not materialize, and the company may soon find itself in financial difficulties. In the worst cases, you may find your own company financing your supplier.

The Business Plan

With a start-up company, nearly the only thing available to analyze is the business plan. There is no previous history of the company's performance. Therefore, the most important existing document should be the business plan. A good business plan is vital to steer the business in the right direction. A good business plan keeps the company out of trouble. The importance of a good business plan is easy to understand if you think about a captain and his ship. To navigate his way to the right port at the right time, a captain needs a map, a schedule, and a compass—nowadays the captain would use the Global Positioning System (GPS). Likewise, in business there must be a destination target and a schedule showing where the business should be at any specific time.

The business plan consists of market potential; competitors; and overall evaluation of the future business, products, technology, financing, and management. One of the most important questions is whether the business plan is fully funded.

Competitors affect the freedom of pricing and the anticipated level of innovations. Tough competition increases the company's difficulties in the market.

The capability of management is important because management makes critical decisions. Evaluating managerial capacity is crucial to understand its ability to make decisions.

It is essential to evaluate the market potential and a company's slice of the market. The company may currently be successful. However, if it cannot invest in new technology, its future market position may start declining. A company cannot live only for the moment; it must think about the future as well.

Qualitative aspects play a more significant role in analyzing start-up companies, and historical quantitative analysis plays a minor role. You need to frequently monitor the development of a start-up company. With the release of every quarterly report, you must determine in which direction the company is headed. If the direction is not correct for your supplier, react quickly.

A business plan should provide sufficient details, and management should be committed to the plan. The business plan should align with a company's vision and strategy.

Key Questions

The most significant questions are marked with an asterisk.

Business Plan

❏ Is the business plan based on realistic assumptions?*
❏ Is the business plan according to the company's vision?*

❑ What is the previous history of the company's business plans? How accurate have they been?*

Growth Companies

In the growth phase, the main target of a company is simply rapidly growing sales volumes. The company must be efficient, and it must have profit targets and straightforward plans to achieve them. During the growth phase, the company reaches the benefits of scale in production. Relative production costs are lower than previously, R&D costs are normally lower as well, and the products are starting to be more visible in the market. The growth phase is positive and normally generates healthy profit margins and increasing cash flows for the company and its investors. After the growth phase, the products reach market saturation. It is essential for the company to find new products or a completely new type of business concept to remain in the market and to keep up the growth. Growth companies need equity funding and debt financing for their growth.

Mature Companies

The signs of the mature phase are the cease of growth in the customer base or even a decline. At the end of the growth phase, competition among rivals increases and price competition intensifies as a result of excess capacity. Sales opportunities are limited to the replacement of products; new innovations to the products are limited. If the company has not found ways to maintain growth in the mature phase, the new approach is even more critical for its future than the traditional approach. In the new approach, the relationship between customer and supplier is closer and their processes are more closely linked. If a company starts to mature, it might affect other companies in the supplier chain. In the traditional approach, price and quality were the driving forces of the supplier relationship. It was easier to change suppliers.

Funds are required for different purposes in the different evaluation phases. A mature company spends funding to rationalize its current production and possibly to find new products.

Declining Companies

After technological changes, a company may find itself in a slower or deeper negative trend with declining or even sharply declining sales and earnings. The positive cash generation turns negative in declining businesses. If the company does not come up with a new formula for doing business in the market, bankruptcy may be the end solution. These companies are hardly innovative and creative because management is spending its time on keeping the company alive.

A declining company needs financing to keep its operations going and to fill the gap that its losses may have generated. A company in the declining phase employs drastic cost-cutting measures and sells off property to avoid financial problems.

Technology

The technology adaptation life cycle in Figure 5-4 illustrates the status of a company's technology.

Innovators

An innovator is a company that creates new innovations. Some of the innovations are useful and will be used by the vast majority. Other innovations will never reach any commercial scale. A company may discover a completely new technology. An innovator is enthusiastic about new technologies. A start-up company is typically an eager innovator. New, innovative technology may be a reason to enter a market.

Figure 5-4. Technology adaptation life cycle.

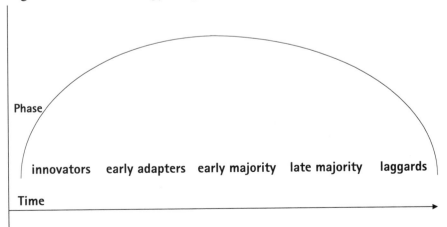

When selecting a supplier, it is essential to consider the balance between innovative technology and risk. R&D departments are eager to incorporate the latest technology into products, but sometimes this technology comes from small start-up companies and they cannot usually fulfill the supplier assessment process. However, to be successful in leading-edge products, sometimes this risk needs to be taken. But the risk needs to be known early in the R&D milestones.

Early Adapters

Early adapters start using the new technology when it is still in its infancy—that is, much earlier than the vast majority. An early adapter is a visionary who is eager to try anything new and wants to be the leader of the pack.

Early Majority

The larger group of users of the new technology is called the early majority. The early majority takes the biggest advantage of the new technology. These users make it a commercial success, and they will succeed themselves. The product flies in the early market, creating a mass market.

Late Majority

The early majority has been using the technology for some time before the late majority accepts the new ideas. In fact, the technology is no longer new; the innovator companies have already lost their interest in the technology. When the late majority starts using the technology, everybody is already familiar with it. The late majority enters the market with conservatism.

Late Adapters

By the time the late adapter (or laggard) wakes up, the innovation has already lost its appeal. The technology is too old even for the early majority, which is now looking for a newer technology to adapt. In that late phase, the late adapters are interested in the technology. Late adapters are the last link in the adaptation life cycle. The innovator has already generated several new ideas when the late adapters are just adopting the previous technology. Late adapters represent a small minority. A declining company that is a late adapter is a dangerous combination. There are few investors interested in investing in declining, late adapters.

Key Questions

The most significant questions are marked with an asterisk.

❑ Which life cycle phase does the supplier company belong to?*

❑ Does your supplier's investment in R&D exceed the industry average?*

If your supplier decreases the dollar amount of R&D investments, how will the company be a top company in the future? R&D investments should result in products and services. Can you see those results?

❑ Does R&D address products in which you are interested?*

If your industry sector typically belongs to the early majority, it is time to consider new businesses. If your industry is in the late majority, there is a rush to consider new businesses.

❑ Are your purchases generally standard items?

❑ Should this type of supplier be in another category?

You cannot expect much innovation and growth if your key suppliers belong to the late majority and laggards. If you, like your investors, value growth, you should limit your supplier selection to the innovator and early adapter companies. These companies are often high-risk companies, but you need to assume some risks to earn profits.

Technology

❑ What are the uncertainties associated with the main technology selected for this company?*

❑ Can this technology be absorbed with the current level of expertise available in the organization?

❑ Does the product mix contain mainly technologically mature products?*

❑ Do competitors have products that will replace the main products of this company?

❑ Is the company developing new future products?

❑ Do the products utilize the newest technology?

❑ Do you need the products representing the new technology?*

Product Portfolio

❑ Has the company concentrated on the products that are the most profitable?*

❑ Does the company have a large production range or only a few products?*

❑ Are the margins too low for these products? How long are the margins expected to be low?

❑ Is the company going to stop producing the products?

❑ What is the competitive advantage of the products and/or services?

❑ What is the quality and price of the products and/or services?

Manufacturing

❑ Is there surplus capacity?

❑ Does the company have room for expansion in its facilities?

❑ How quick and easy is it to expand capacity?*

❑ Is the company producing at full capacity but still generating losses?*

❑ Can the machinery and equipment be leased?

❑ How quickly can the company make investments?

Ownership

Companies can be privately or publicly owned. Based on its ownership base, a company can be a sole proprietorship, a partnership, or a corporation. The different ownership structure is based on the responsibilities of the owners and the size of the company.

Privately Owned Companies

There are usually relatively few shareholders in a privately owned company. Privately owned companies are typically small or middle size and the main owners are often in the top management and frequently involved in the daily business. The funding of a privately owned company is mostly based on the owners' ability to finance the company and bank financing.

Sole Proprietorship

A sole proprietorship is typically for small businesses. The owner also maintains the financial responsibility. A sole proprietorship is easy to create because the business is owned and managed by one individual. It is the most popular form of business ownership. The sole proprietorship does not need large investments.

Partnership

Partnerships are easy to establish. They are based on a partnership agreement, which specifies the division of profits. A partnership is a commonly used structure in Germany, for example. The capital base can be large or limited. The capital base is larger in a partnership than it is in a sole proprietorship, and the responsibility and profits are shared.

Family-Owned Business

Family-owned businesses are owned and controlled by one family.

One or a Few Main Owners with Limited Resources

In this category of business, the owners have often established the company and created the business idea. In some cases, they are good at creating businesses; however, their skills may be limited in managing a quickly growing company.

If the company is privately owned with some entrepreneurs, it normally has a more restricted possibility to grow quickly because the share capital is limited and the owner sometimes cannot increase the capital significantly. The company has limited possibilities to invest. If the company has invested heavily, it has possibly incurred debt financing. If the indebtedness of the company is high, the loan margin increases along with the fear of financial problems.

Main Owner Is Managing Director

Risk is high in companies in which the owner is also the managing director. If something happens to him or her, what will happen to the company? The company is too dependent on one person. Often an entrepreneur is innovative and can run a company very well. However, the difficulty might emerge when the company needs to grow quickly. The company may lack managerial and financial resources. The limited amount of management skills may cause inefficiency. Some companies can manage this phase well and continue their growth. Other companies struggle. The worst case occurs when the company loses the advantages of being a small and effective company but does not grow to become a large and effective company.

When the main owner is the managing director, the company can:

Strengthening Factors

❑ Be creative, if the entrepreneur is creative.

❑ Have quick decision making because the management team is small.

Weakening Factors

❑ Be stagnate, if the entrepreneur is stagnate.

❑ Have limited financial resources, if the owner cannot invest in the company.

Private Equity Organizations—Venture Capitalists as Owners

Private equity organizations finance high-risk, potentially high-reward projects: start-up companies requiring substantial capital and troubled companies needing to undergo restructuring. The typical features of a start-up company are negative earnings for some years and uncertain prospects, which create uncertainty in receiving bank loans or other debt financing. The troubled companies might face the same difficulty when attempting to raise external financing.

The company can be a privately held company, in which the main owner is a private equity organization or several equity organizations. Private equity organizations are willing to invest in business that is higher risk with high reward expectations in the future. They see the possibility of growth, and very often, quick growth.

Private equity organizations can take part in the strategy creation. They can add the missing pieces to make the company profitable, but they may also lose the original strengths of the company. The original entrepreneur may lose interest in the company, and in time, he or she might not care about the success of the company. In those circumstances, the company needs new owners.

Private equity organizations raise funds from institutions and individuals. The purpose of a private equity organization is often to gain a quick profit. Therefore, only in limited cases can you expect them to make a long-term investment in the company. This situation may arise, for example, if a private equity organization has similar types of companies in the same branch or with a similar business idea, and the companies can add value to each other.

If the main owner is a private equity organization, take into consideration the following issues:

Strengthening Factors

❑ Financial support from venture capitalists

❑ Support for the original business idea and entrepreneurship

Weakening Factors

❑ Quick gains for venture capitalists

❑ Dismissal of the original business idea and entrepreneurship

Publicly Owned Companies

There are normally a number of shareholders in publicly owned corporations. In corporations, the liability of the stockholders is limited to their investment in the company. If none of the owners holds a significant amount of the shares, the management of the company generally has substantial decision-making power.

In general, the management of publicly owned companies has a stronger position in decision making, and the company has larger financial resources to potentially collect funds through public offerings.

Key Questions

The most significant questions are marked with an asterisk.

Ownership

❑ Who are the main owners?*

❑ Do the owners have the capacity to invest in the company in the future?*

❑ If the company is a start-up and privately owned, how successful have the owners' previous investments been?

❑ If the owner is a venture capitalist, what is its investment history?

❑ How long can the owner/owners withstand losses?*

❑ What is the owner's main interest in the company?

❑ Is the company doing business with a company owned by the same owner(s) as this company?

Corporate Structure

The corporate structure is chosen in the corporate strategy. An advantage might be gained by grouping separate businesses together. The corporate structure can be simple and clear or it can be complicated. It is easy to understand and analyze the companies with a clear structure. Outsiders—such as bankers, investors, suppliers, tax authorities, and customers—can easily find the performance of the company. A complicated company structure may be created to hide the "real" operational result from outsiders.

One of the main reasons for a complicated company structure is to avoid taxes. Another way to escape taxes is to have the offshore headquarters located in tax heaven such as Bermuda or the Cayman Islands.

The essential parts of analyzing ownership are:

❑ The risk and benefits the owners bring to the company

❑ The owners' possibilities and willingness to financially support the company and its subsidiaries

The typical structure of ownership varies in different countries. In Germany, blocks are often held by other companies—a cross-holding of shares—or by holding companies for families.

The term *keiretsu*, which is used in Japan, means a network of companies, usually organized around a major bank. There are long-standing business relationships among the group companies; a manufacturing company might buy a substantial part of its raw materials from group suppliers, and in turn, sell much of its output to other group companies. The banks and other financial institutions at the core of the *keiretsu* own shares in most of the group companies.

Holding Companies

There may be a holding company or a pyramid of holding companies controlling other holding companies. A holding company's structure is presented in Figure 5-5. A pyramid of holding companies, in which a holding company is owned by another holding company, is presented in Figure 5-6. In that case, a company can have several subsidiaries or the same owner can own several interrelated companies. The possibility of earnings and losses is greater, as is the leverage of risk, in holding companies. A loss by one subsidiary might be magnified.

Figure 5-5. A holding company structure.

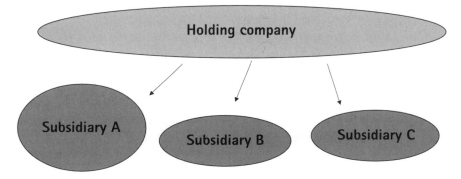

Figure 5-6. Pyramid of holding companies.

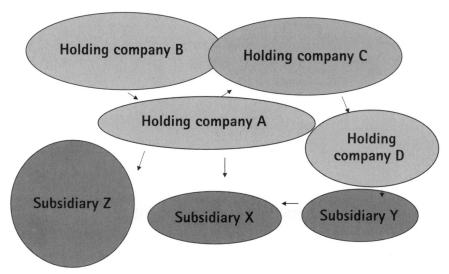

The advantage of holding companies is the leverage effect that permits the company to control a large amount of assets with relatively small investment and risk.

A holding company is a company that has voting control of one or more other corporations. The company may need to own only a small percentage of the outstanding shares to have this voting control. A full 100 percent ownership is not needed to control the other companies.

A holding company can be a parent company, which only keeps holdings and does not have any business itself.

Subsidiaries

Large companies often own other companies that are part of their business activities. A corporation that owns other businesses is the *parent company,* and the owned companies are called *subsidiaries.* Figure 5-7 shows a parent company and its subsidiaries.

The combined financial statements of the parent company and its subsidiaries are called the consolidated financial statements. The need to present consolidated financial statements depends on the share of the ownership. Consolidated financial statements were discussed in Chapter 4.

The BCD Ltd. company in Ireland has incurred losses. The debt ratio (debts to total assets) is high. The company's liabilities are too high.

Figure 5-7. Parent company and its subsidiaries.

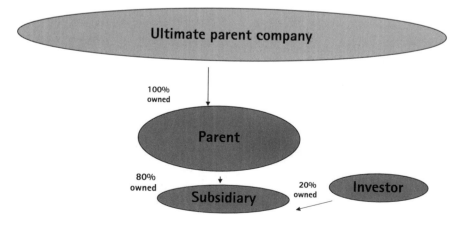

The company BCD Inc. is listed on the NYSE; it has a long and stable history. BCD Inc. owns 100 percent of BCD Ltd. in Ireland. The parent company has financed the subsidiary. The company in Ireland is concentrating on getting more market share in Ireland and Britain, and the marketing costs are high.

Don't stop your investigation at this point! Take a credit report or a who-owns-whom report. You may find that your supplier is a subsidiary of the large U.S.-listed company BCD Inc.

You must analyze the consolidated financial figures of the group to obtain a better understanding of the company's potential. The parent company can finance the subsidiary, or, if the subsidiary is not profitable enough, the parent company might sell the subsidiary.

An ordinary rule of thumb when evaluating companies is that the subsidiary cannot obtain a better rating than its parent company. If the parent company sells the subsidiary, you might be interested in who the new owner is.

Key Questions

The most significant questions are marked with an asterisk.

Company Structure

❑ What is the company structure?*

❑ Does the company structure include holding companies?*

Subsidiaries

❑ Does the company have subsidiaries?*

❑ If so, how many subsidiaries?

❑ In which countries are the subsidiaries located?

❑ When was the subsidiary established? A newly established subsidiary may need financial support from the parent company.

❑ Does the company and its subsidiaries have consolidated financial figures or only separate financial statements? If the related companies have separate financial statements, they might have significant internal trade, making it impossible for an outsider to estimate the real profitability of the company.

❑ Does the company and its subsidiaries have internal trade? To what extent?

❑ What are the overall goals of the parent company?*

❑ What is the strategic importance of this subsidiary to the parent company?*

❑ What are the current results of the subsidiary?

❑ Why did the parent get into this business?

Organization

The structure of an organization is chosen by top management. The approach to organizational structure can be presented as follows:

❑ Functional structure

❑ Divisional structure

❑ Mixed structure, called a matrix organization

The organizational structure should serve the business; it should support the business in reaching its targets.

❑ *Functional structure* is divided into functions, for example, marketing, production, finance, purchasing, and R&D. Each function concentrates on its own special elements and the function is controlled by the head of that function.

❑ *Divisional structure* is based on the existence of separate divisions and their individual strategies. Divisions can be divided according to geographical areas or business areas. Each division has its own function, such as finance, marketing, purchasing, or human resources.

❑ *Matrix structure* has two dimensions involving the head of different divisions and cross-organizational teams.

A company should choose the organizational structure that best serves its corporate strategy in the changing business environment.

Key Questions

The most significant questions are marked with an asterisk.

Divisions

❑ Does the company have several divisions?*

❑ What is the future focus of the company?*

❑ Which business area is the future core business of your supplier?

❑ Are you interested in the products belonging to the future focus business?

❑ Are the products you are interested in the products of a division that will probably be sold?*

❑ Who will possibly buy that division?

Organization

❑ Is the organization flexible or formal?*

❑ Are authority and responsibility relationships clearly established?

Management

Managerial competence is a key issue of a successful company. Managerial inexperience and poor decision making are the main problems of a failing enterprise. A large company may not fail completely, but poor management can be fatal to a small company.

Especially in smaller companies, management may lack experience, the board may have little input into decision making, and the business is a one-person show. In large companies, top management rarely lacks experience. However, the board may be an ineffective administrative team and may be too large or the finance function may have a weak position in the company. Experience consists of the following elements: the ability to coordinate, manage, and motivate people; technical ability; and the power to visualize and integrate the various operations into a synergistic whole.

The organization reflects top management's ideas on how the company should work. The capability of top management is essential. In corporate analysis, top management should be evaluated. Some issues to evaluate include top management's competence, reputation, experience, education, and knowledge of the field. The cooperation of top management with owners and investors is key to the success of a company. To assess the quality of management as part of the review process is an essential part of analysis.

The analysis of the organization and management should evaluate the competencies of top management, the effectiveness of the organization, and reporting and control systems.

Key Questions

The most significant questions are marked with an asterisk.

Management

❏ Does management have experience in this type of business?*

❏ What is the management team's background?*

❏ Is the background of the management team haunted by past bankruptcies, or does it have any skeletons in the closet related to fraudulent activities?

❏ If management has been involved in a bankruptcy, what was the reason for the bankruptcy?

The reason might be the inability to be in the market, too quick growth, or lack of management skills.

❏ Do some top management members have a reputation for strong experience in management or in creating technology or start-up companies?

❏ Does management have the adequate education and skills for this business?

❏ Is the company newly established, and the management team inexperienced and young?

The company might be innovative but there is a substantial managerial risk.

❏ Are those in management young (in their twenties) or very senior (in their sixties and seventies)?

❏ Are the older members releasing enough power to the newcomers?

❏ Are the newcomers taking too much power and dismissing the old, good ideas?

❏ How capable is management at making changes?*

❏ Is the board monitoring the executive management?*

Acquisitions and Mergers

The wave of acquisitions reached a peak from 1999 to 2000. The growing companies were looking for critical skills they didn't have themselves or for the missing parts of the business. However, the success of mergers and acquisitions depends on several factors, such as the match between the companies' business climates, the combination of knowledge and expertise, and—one of the most critical factors—employee willingness to cooperate. Employees readily change jobs when they do not feel comfortable in the new business climate after a merger. In some cases, the company that has made the acquisition finds the "real" value of its investment—that is, the skilled workforce—ready to leave the company.

You should carefully evaluate the consequences of acquisitions. Was the acquisition based on realistic assumptions? The heavy wave of acquisitions left many inflated balance sheets. The stocks dropped their values dramatically and the growth prospects were cut down.

Key Questions

The most significant questions are marked with an asterisk.

Acquisitions

❑ Has the company made any acquisitions during the past two years?

❑ If the company has made several acquisitions, how have the acquisitions affected the company's financial statement?*

❑ Has there been a significant amount of amortization of goodwill and restructuring costs?*

❑ Is the company going to make any acquisitions this year?

Executive Summary

A SWOT analysis is generally used for identifying an organization's strengths, weaknesses, opportunities, and threats. A SWOT analysis can also be used in an executive summary. The need to highlight different areas of the analysis depends on several factors, such as the level of supplier relationship: Is the supplier an existing supplier or a new supplier? Is the supplier an existing company with a longer business history or is it a start-up company? The indebtedness of the planned relationship should also be taken into account: Is it a question of a deep supplier relationship such as outsourcing or is it a short-term relationship with relatively low purchasing volumes?

Key Questions

The most significant questions are marked with an asterisk.

Recommendations

❑ Are there some special features of the company?

❑ Are you concerned about the company in some specific area such as financing, technology, markets, or management?*

❑ What has been the trend of the financial figures? Why?*

❑ If the company has made significant acquisitions in the recent past, do you estimate that the acquisitions have been successful and will support the business in the future or maybe not at all?

❑ Would you recommend this supplier as a partner for your company in every case? For small purchases only? Never? Why?*

❑ Do you suspect that the supplier needs your company's support? Is your company ready to support the supplier? If so, in what way? Technologically (by offering some R&D support), financially (through prepayments or taking part in investments), or in some other way?

Business Failure

After analyzing the qualitative and quantitative factors of a company, you may discover the elements of a possible business failure. An unfavorable outcome of business activities is called a business failure. A company may fail because its returns are negative or low. If a company consistently reports operating losses, it will probably experience a decline in market value. If a company fails to earn a return that is greater than its cost of capital, it can be viewed as having a failure. It is more possible that a company files for bankruptcy when the operations of the company are unprofitable. However, not every unprofitable company goes bankrupt. As long as the company can gather enough cash to pay the interest on its debt, it may be able to postpone bankruptcy for many years. Eventually the company may recover, pay off its debt, and escape bankruptcy altogether.

A major cause of business failure is mismanagement. There is never any need for fear of overemphasizing the importance of capable management. Numerous specific managerial faults can cause a company to fail. Some that are worth mentioning include overexpansion, poor financial actions, ineffective sales force, and high production costs—all of which can singly or in combination cause failure.

It is rare that insolvency or bankruptcy hits without warning. The first phase of insolvency is technical insolvency. It occurs when a company is unable to pay its liabilities as they come due. When a company is technically insolvent, its assets are still greater than its liabilities, but it encounters a liquidity crisis.

The second phase of insolvency is bankruptcy. It occurs when a company's liabilities exceed the fair market value of its assets. A bankrupt company has a negative shareholders' equity. Even in the second phase of insolvency, a company can avoid bankruptcy if the company agrees on a repayment program with its financiers and/or if the owners of the company are willing to invest in the company.

Qualitative Factors—Issues for Special Attention

❑ Look at the history of the company. Remember that a company in business less than three years has a higher probability of bankruptcy.

❑ Analyze changes. Be concerned about resignations or changes in executive management, and significant changes in the company's business.

❑ Remember that all changes take time. New management normally needs time to change the direction of the company.

❑ Be aware that all acquisitions won't be profitable and successful for the acquiring company.

❑ Be aware of the company's chances of finding external additional financing.

❑ Pay attention if the company in a declining industry is growing fast.

❑ Check for possible lawsuits, outstanding litigation, liens or judgments and determine if there is a threat of material impact.

Key Points

Environment

❑ The environment creates the circumstances for a company. A company cannot be handled out of its environment.

❑ *Political environment* includes the rules and regulations the government implements as well as changes in government. A change in government or an unstable political climate may present challenges to a company.

❑ *Regulatory environment,* such as laws and requirements, creates the frame within which business is conducted. Changes in the regulatory environment affect a company's business.

❑ *Market and competitors.* A company can be a market leader, but the market in every sector affects the company. Competition exists in every open market. As the market matures, the competition gets tougher. A company might have several competitors based on location—local and global competitors—or based on size—small, medium, and large companies.

❑ *Customers* are interested in a company's products. A company must offer desirable products to its customers. A marketing strategy is a vital way to reach customers.

❑ *Suppliers and logistics* are important for production and deliveries. A customer will not get the delivery as promised if the suppliers are incapable of meeting their deliveries and the logistics chain is dysfunctional. You need to ensure that the companies delivering to your suppliers are competent companies in their own area.

Corporate

❑ Strategy is a key part of a company's existence.

Like humans, companies experience different types of phases in their life cycles. The phases can be summarized as follows:

❑ *Start-up phase.* The risk for survival is high.

❑ *Growth phase.* The risk is still relatively high, but the company already has a background and its products or services are starting to be better known.

❑ *Maturity phase.* The company has a history so it is easy to evaluate its past and forecast its future. However, the company may fall into the declining phase.

❑ *Declining phase.* The company is struggling to live and to turn the decline into new growth. Some companies manage to return to growth by finding new products and services or by substantially improving the current products and services. Some companies file for bankruptcy and go out of business.

The business plan is the plan arising from strategy. It covers the market potential, competitors, and overall evaluation of the future business, products, technology, financing, and management. One of the most important questions arising is whether the business plan is fully funded.

❑ *Technology* consists of the technology or technologies the company is using and its products are supporting. Companies can be classified according to their style of involvement with new technologies. The categories are innovators, early adapters, early majority, late majority, and laggards.

❑ *Ownership* affects a company's needs concerning publicity and the requirements to publish its financial results. Ownership of the company may also support or hinder the accessibility to outside financing. A publicly owned company has strict requirements to complete and publish its financial statements. A privately owned company might not have any requirements about publishing its financial statements. The regulations concerning privately owned companies and the publication of financial information vary from country to country.

❑ *Management* and its competence is a key factor for business success. Managerial inexperience and poor decision making are the main problems of the failing enterprise.

Company Structure

❑ The *company structure* can be simple and clear or, conversely, very complicated. If there is only one legal entity, or if all subsidiaries and affiliates are consolidated to the financial statements, it is easy for outsiders to find the real financial performance of the company.

❑ Through a *holding company or a pyramid of holding companies*, an owner can control a group of companies with lower investments and risk. In holding companies, the possibility of earnings and losses, as well as the leverage of risks, is greater. A loss by one subsidiary may be magnified.

❑ A *subsidiary* may be owned 100 percent or less by the parent company. If the parent company owns 100 percent of the subsidiary, total control belongs to the parent company.

❑ *Organization* can effectively support the business or be a hindrance to the business.

❑ *Acquisitions and mergers* create additional requirements affecting the business operations. Several acquisitions over a short time may later cause the need to downsize the company.

Executive Summary

❑ *An executive summary* points out the strengths, weaknesses, opportunities, and threats of the company. An executive summary is based on the findings of quantitative and qualitative factors of the company. Recommendations are given based on the SWOT and overall view of the company.

Business Failure

❑ An unfavorable outcome of business activities is business failure. A company might fail because its returns are negative or low, rendering it unable to meet its creditor's requirements on time.

Conclusions of Part One and Part Two

The need and extent of analyzing your suppliers depends on several factors, including your risk strategy and objectives in purchasing and operations, your operational strategy in purchasing, the significance of the supplier, and the resources available to make the analysis:

Your strategy to take risks in purchasing and operations. If you are willing to take high risks in purchasing and operations, there is no need to analyze your suppliers.

Operational strategy in purchasing. Suppliers for standard products are relatively easy to replace with another supplier. The replacement of suppliers for specific commodities normally takes longer. You need to make a comprehensive analysis or at least a short analysis of the suppliers that are difficult to replace, if you do not want to take high risks in sourcing.

Significance of the supplier. An important driver when deciding on the extent of analysis is the definition of focused supplier. A focused supplier directly affects the competitive advantage of a company. Focused suppliers should be analyzed by making a corporate analysis or short analysis. Supplier risk is the driving force behind specifying the type of analysis that is made of the suppliers. If the potential loss is high, the supplier analysis should be more comprehensive.

Resources. The style and depth of the analysis requires people to analyze suppliers. If purchasing managers are analyzing their suppliers themselves, it is recommended to start with a short analysis. The comprehensive analysis is more feasible when business controllers, or dedicated people in the company, are analyzing the suppliers.

Summary

It is recommended that companies conduct a corporate analysis of key suppliers for specific commodities, for example, those that are difficult to replace with another supplier in the short term. The existing risk level is high.

Financial analysis should be made of the suppliers with middle or low risk. Your willingness to take risks will further define the target group.

Case 4: A Publicly Owned Large Company

Jill Turner and the assessment team were sitting in the small meeting room. She counted twelve people: seven from Success Inc. and five from the supplier's side. She listened as a middle-aged man with dark hair told them, "Our factories are ideally situated compared to our competitors. We have several locations in Europe, Asia, and, of course, America." He moved quickly to the wall and showed a new white building on the screen. He looked directly into Jill's eyes and continued proudly, "This is our newest factory in Mexico. We acquired it from XXX Ltd. last month. You'll find the details in our press release in the files I gave you."

The man spoke fluently, pointing out some words and repeating them from time to time. "Excellent locations" was one of those phrases he repeated. He was an above-average speaker but his presentation was not the best Jill had ever heard. His eyes were dark and cold.

He looked at all of them, one by one, but he never hesitated, not once. Jill imagined him giving a presentation to the press. He had given several during his career. Jill looked at her coworkers. All of them were men, middle-aged and older. Some of them looked focused as they listened to the presentation; others were looking at the files they had been given. Jill sighed and looked at her list of questions on the table. "Do I have answers for all the open items? What is still missing?" She tried to look at the questions while following what the man was saying. Jill looked at him occasionally but turned her eyes to her questions.

Next to the tall man was a slimmer, dark-haired English man, who was the technical adviser of Supplier A. He looked bored. Suddenly, his eyes snapped open. A question about technical detail had been asked by Jill's coworker, seated next to her. The dark-haired English man cleared his throat as he moved forward in his chair, starting to formulate his answer.

"That is a very good question. I agree that many companies have not thought it through thoroughly but we have spent a lot of time studying the possibilities of quick changes in production lines. I am really proud of the work our team has done. If you want to have more details, please don't hesitate to give me a call."

The man paused for a breath and continued. The other man was quiet as he sat down. Quite odd, Jill thought. Why are they not speaking? The light-haired Swedish controller had not said a word. His gaze slowly turned to the walls. He sighed from time to time. Jill stopped looking at the men and tried to concentrate on the presentation. A quick glance at her watch showed that it had already gone on for nearly two hours without a break. Some had asked questions, but mostly the man just talked on and on: ". . . last year sales increased 90 percent compared to a year ago. We are very proud of the achievement. This year the growth has continued at the same speed . . ."

Suddenly, the door of the small room opened. It was located opposite of Jill. Everybody turned to face the door.

"I apologize for being late," said a Finnish man. "May I present our senior vice president of operations, Mr. Jarmo Kallio." Mr. Kallio smiled as he firmly shook hands with all the representatives of the potential supplier.

Mr. Kallio sat next to Jill, the only seat available. Jill had not seen Mr. Kallio many times and he did not recognize her. Jill looked at her questions more carefully as Mr. Kallio took his place. Unlike the others, he did not take his coat off.

The discussion was livelier than before, with Mr. Kallio asking many questions in a loud voice. One of the questions, which Jill knew already, was for all potential suppliers.

"I would still like to ask you something," Mr. Kallio looked squarely at the man who was giving the presentation. Everybody caught their breath. "Has this meeting given you what you expected?"

The man took a step forward, put his left hand to his face, thought for a moment, and then answered, "Well, I think this is pretty much what we expected." The tone of his voice was quicker than before. He ran his fingers through his hair.

"What did he expect from us, that we place an order right away, be more cooperative?" he thought.

Mr. Kallio proceeded in a friendly manner, "I would like to get frank answers; do you expect something more from us? Should we know more? Have we asked good questions? Should we provide you with more information?" Mr. Kallio leaned forward and folded his hands as he and the whole team kept a steady gaze on the man at the podium. The man moved again. He had collected himself, remembering many of the press conferences he had been to and the unexpected, sometimes impolite, questions.

"Your questions have been very good and I think that we have also learned a lot. I hope that we can be your partner in the future. If you want to know something, we would be happy to provide you with more information. We can ask some of our current customers if they would talk with you and provide you with more information about the way we conduct business."

Jill looked excitedly at Mr. Kallio. His round face was back to normal and it looked as though he didn't expect a longer answer. The answer was polite but did not reveal anything. No emotional feeling, nothing. There was no more coming. Mr. Kallio knew that. He was busy, as vice presidents normally are.

Mr. Kallio stood up and politely thanked all the representatives of the potential supplier. "I apologize, but I have to leave; my schedule is tight today. I am very pleased to have met you and now I'll let our team continue."

Jill skimmed through the articles that were included in the files that the representatives of the potential supplier had given them. "We will be number one in the industry," claimed the headline. Jill stared at the person in the picture: It was the man at the podium. Jill glanced at the business cards in front of her and at their titles, "CEO, President of Supplier A Inc., Robert E. Jones." Nowadays, there are several vice presidents, senior vice presidents, and presidents in companies. Jill had not spent much time studying the business cards. That was a mistake and she knew it. She had to find the right people to answer her questions.

Robert E. Jones continued his presentation. Jill glanced down at her questions. Robert E. Jones had answered almost all the questions but she still found some new ones. Jill shifted slightly in her chair. She waited a moment before starting. Jill wondered if her voice would be loud enough. Jill's coworker, the bold technical specialist, had stopped his questions. Jill thought her time had come. She cleared her throat.

Everybody stared at her. She didn't mind. "Could you please let me know the ownership of your company? What is the purpose of the holding company in the Cayman Islands? Where is the headquarters, in the United States or in the Cayman Islands?" Jill looked at Robert E. Jones firmly.

Robert E. Jones looked at her directly and smiled. Jill saw that he had been asked those questions several times before. He was prepared. "Our headquarters is in the Cayman Islands for tax reasons, but our company is listed on NASDAQ in the United States. Our main production facilities are located in California. I could very much say that our company is an American state with lower taxes, which naturally benefits our customers." He smiled and waited for signs that the answer was good enough for Jill. She considered this information thoughtfully and wrote down some remarks.

Jill disliked overly complicated company structures. Those companies were difficult to analyze. The truth behind the profitability was concealed. The few owners might manage the entire company group with low investments. Jill continued asking more questions about ownership. "Who is that American investor mentioned in your annual report?" Robert E. Jones either did not know or did not want to reveal the name. Jill learned that the company would publish its financial figures in two days, so she discontinued her questions for the time being. Bad timing for the visit. Jill smiled and thanked him.

That was almost the end of the meeting. They all stood up, shook hands again, and said thank-you. The men were leaving. Jill was puzzled by something and turned to her coworker: "Why didn't the other people say anything?"

"Well, would you talk while our president gave a presentation?"

"I doubt it," Jill answered thoughtfully.

Robert E. Jones gave Success Inc. all the information it wanted via e-mail. His presentation was good and promising; the company was a solid, listed company. The company structure was slightly complicated, but not overly complicated compared to the large size of the company. Supplier A got the deal.

Case 5: A Small Privately Owned Company with a Complicated Structure

"Are these companies subsidiaries of Creative Works Ltd.?" asked purchasing manager Leslie Smith in her e-mail message. After the question, she had listed ten names. All of them were somewhat strange. Jill had not heard of any of them before. Jill forwarded the file to her assistant, Renate Stadelmann, and asked her to get credit information on all the companies.

Jill was still reading some of her e-mail when the telephone next to her rang. "Jill Turner," she answered.

"Hi, Jill. It's me." Jill heard the familiar voice. "Guess what?" Jill was reading an e-mail while she was talking with Renate on the telephone.

"I give up, Renate."

"You have lovely companies," she told her in a teasing voice.

"What do you mean?" Jill wanted her to speak directly and to drop the guessing game.

Renate replied, "You asked about companies that don't exist!"

"What do you mean? Didn't you find any credit information? That doesn't necessarily mean that the companies don't exist," Jill sounded perturbed.

Renate was laughing. "There wasn't any information about these companies. Are these companies our suppliers or potential suppliers?" Renate asked.

"Those companies may be subsidiaries of our supplier."

"What is the name of the supplier?"

"Creative Works Ltd., in e-business."

"Those companies are sometimes strange," Renate advised Jill. "I'll let you know if I find more information about the companies." Renate ended the phone call.

Several days had passed since the request for the analysis of Creative Works Ltd. Jill had a meeting with them. The purchasing manager told Jill that the wife of the managing director and main owner, a director herself in Creative Works Ltd., would come with her husband.

Jim and Hanna Ashworth approached them as they arrived at the hall. They knew Jill's colleague by sight. They had met several times before.

The lawyer of Success Inc., a young woman wearing shoes that matched her dress, came into the meeting room. They were ready to start the meeting and get to the questions. Purchasing manager Leslie Smith; Jill; and their lawyer, Nina Strand, sat opposite the door. The Ashworths had their backs to the door.

Leslie Smith opened the meeting: "We are currently negotiating a long-term contract with you." Jim Ashworth was nodding. Hanna Ashworth was sighing and staring at John with her big blue eyes.

"Yes, we are negotiating, definitely," confirmed Jim.

Leslie continued, "We used to make a corporate analysis of all our significant suppliers. That's why we have asked you to come here today."

Hanna stared at Leslie for a moment. Jim nodded.

"Jill and Nina are here today to make an assessment of your company's capability to be our supplier. Jill is from the finance and controlling department and Nina is from the legal department."

Hanna smiled slightly. Jim opened his mouth but didn't say anything.

Leslie turned to Jill and Nina. "Please start." It couldn't have been a more painful start. Jill quickly looked at Nina. She gave a slight nod to Jill to indicate that Jill could start.

"Could you please explain to us the following companies: Happy Eyes Pty, Laughing Eyes Pty, Smiling Face Ltd, Because Inc., Coughing Bear Ltd, Silly Dog Inc., Creative Jeopardy Ltd, Serious Ltd, Deliver Me Ltd, Trust Me SA, and Happy with You Ltd."

Jill looked at Jim straight on. He was in his midforties and had black hair and a stony face. Hanna shifted in her chair. She turned to Jim but didn't say anything. Jim remained silent for a long time. Then he started to answer.

"The companies that you mentioned are our partners."

"Do you own your partners?" Jill continued with her questioning.

"Our partners are independent companies," Jim replied in a slow and frank voice.

"Could you please still specify your relationship with the companies? You don't own them. Who does own these companies?" Jill pressed on.

Hanna licked her lips and moved forward and back.

"We co-operate with those companies," replied Jim in an even louder voice.

"Jill means who owns the companies? Do you know who owns your close partners?" helped Nina, continuing the questioning. Nina was close to thirty and wore an expensive-looking necklace. Nobody could mistake that she was a lawyer, a very talented lawyer—even if she was young.

Hanna held her hand to her lips. "Jim, can you remember anything about our partners?" she asked softly.

"Maybe, it would be easiest to start with the company Happy Eyes Pty," Jill said, studying the long list of names.

"Happy Eyes Pty is a Czech company. I think it was established at least ten years ago," Jim replied.

"Do you know the owners of the company?" Jill insisted firmly.

"We haven't co-operated with the company during the past year. I don't remember much about the company. Do you, Hanna? You've visited it," Jim said and turned to Hanna.

"Nice people in that company. I don't know who owns the company," Hanna answered smiling. "I can ask them if you wish to know," she proceeded in a friendly tone.

"That would be really nice," Jill said, moving on to the next name: Laughing Eyes Pty.

Hanna turned to Jim, "You must know that company, don't you?" she asked with a begging voice.

"We have worked with Laughing Eyes Pty for several years. It is a good company," Jim answered.

"Who are the owners?" Jill emphasized.

"Some Russian businesspeople. They have several other businesses, too." Jim replied nervously.

"Which line of business are their other businesses in?" Jill asked.

"They have multiple lines of business," Jim confirmed in a dark voice.

"Do they own Laughing Eyes Pty themselves?"

"I am not sure. The owners have several holding companies," Jim replied. It was easy to hear the increasing tightness in his voice. "Can we get to the details of the contract?" he said, narrowing his eyes.

"Not yet. I think that Nina and Jill still have some questions to ask. The ownership of your partners is not yet clear," Leslie said firmly.

Jim and Hanna Ashworth glanced at each other. Was the meeting turning out more difficult than they had expected? They had not imagined that the representatives of Success Inc. would be interested in their partners. They tried to cover the area of ownership of their partners as lightly as possible: Nobody else had shown such great interest in their partners.

Jill later found out that Happy Eyes Pty was established only a few months earlier—not ten years ago. The company Coughing Bear Ltd had declared bankruptcy; Trust Me Pty was founded four years ago but the line of business was different than expected.

Case 6: A Start-Up Company

Jill's flight from Great Britain to the United States was delayed almost twelve hours. It was 4 A.M. in Cleveland. Almost lunchtime in London. She had four hours before her breakfast meeting with Ross, the sourcing manager of Success Inc. Jill slept like a rock.

At 8:30, Jill was at the breakfast table wearing the same black, rumpled T-shirt she had been wearing since leaving Great Britain more than thirty hours ago. Her hair was wet and messy. The breakfast buffet was generous: bacon, eggs, cornflakes, yogurt, muffins, etc. She chose bacon, eggs, fried tomatoes, and mushrooms with a large glass of orange juice and a big blueberry muffin. Ross came in wearing a white shirt and black suit.

"Hi, Jill," he said as he approached. "I thought that something had happened because you were not at the hotel when I checked in last night."

"I had difficulties with my flight." After the full story of the journey, they went into details about the company.

"Here is the technology roadmap." Ross took out a PowerPoint slide.

"You see, here is this point of the process. We thought about using the new technology of PP Inc. to compensate for the older technology in this area."

"According to the short financial analysis I made, the financial figures don't look too good—a loss by now," Ross continued.

"I saw the short financial analysis and the figures were alarming in many ways," Jill stated, glancing at Ross. "I also made the corporate analysis as a desk study, which I sent to you, too. It was not possible to get answers to all the open questions by only using the external sources," Jill continued.

"Yes, I know," Ross commented. "It is your business to find out if PP Inc. has the strength to grow with us." Ross studied Jill, but Jill hardly could see him through her disheveled hair. As she pushed her hair away from her face, she could smell body odor on her shirt.

"Let's go. We can go shopping first if you'd like to buy something for your kids. How old are they?" Ross asked.

"Einari is four months old and Heidi is six years old."

"We'll find something for them," Ross said warmly. "After the short shopping round, we'll go have lunch. The company does not have its own cafeteria. They will not be offering us lunch. We'd better eat before we go."

After changing her clothes, Jill returned to the lobby and met Ross. They traveled to the site in a rental car.

They soon found the low, white building that served as PP Inc.'s headquarters. There was construction work going on behind it. "The new factory?" Jill asked, stepping out of the car.

"The last time I visited, the building wasn't as far along. They've made a lot of progress in the last two months," Ross stated thoughtfully.

"Ross, have you been here many times before?"

"Too often, I think. Maybe ten times."

"This is your company!" Jill said cheerfully.

"Yeah. I am the newest one on our team. I got PP Inc., the most complicated company for us," Ross laughed.

"Ross, you may be the smartest one, too, because you have a university degree in economics and engineering." Ross blushed and they walked into the building.

The woman at the reception desk was in her midforties, with short curly hair. "Our host is Eric Silvio."

The woman picked up the telephone and called Eric Silvio, chair of PP Inc. "Your guests are here," she said in a hesitating voice. "Please sit down, Mr. Silvio will be here in a moment."

Jill let her eyes wander from one corner to another in the small and sparsely furnished reception room. The decorations were plain, without any special interest. "Hi, Ross. Nice to see you again," Eric appeared, smiling and extending his hands. Eric was in his late forties, with a bald head and a round face. He was wearing horn-rimmed glasses and a signature button-down dress shirt—unusual clothes for a man who normally wore a T-shirt at the office.

"Jill Turner."

"Nice to meet you, Jill. Please come in. All our board members are already present in our boardroom," Eric continued. They walked through some corridors in the white-walled factory building. The boardroom was on the second floor. Eric opened the door to a dark room with a large, dominating brown table. There were three men and one woman already in the room. Jill shook hands with all of them and exchanged business cards. They sat down. Ross was sitting next to her.

"The most important person today is Jill. She will make a corporate analysis, which is a normal process in our supplier selection. A corporate analysis consists of quantitative and qualitative parts and it supports our supplier selection," Ross opened the meeting on behalf of Success Inc. All the participants looked at Jill and nodded. "We want to really know the companies with which we are dealing. Jill, please ask your questions," Ross said, turning to her.

Jill had arranged her belongings on the table, including her list of questions. Six pairs of eyes were staring at her. This was not Jill's first meeting. She looked at her preliminary questions. Part one—the company.

"Who currently owns PP Inc.?"

Eric and Dexter looked at each other.

"Dexter, you have the newest information on our owners." Dexter Taylor, senior vice president of finance and treasury and public relations, folded his hands in front of him and looked at Jill firmly.

"VVP Inc. is still our largest shareholder with a 40 percent shareholding."

"Is VVP in the same line of business as your company?" Jill asked.

Eric raised his voice. "VVP is our main owner but we do not compete with each other."

"You do have the same products," Ross observed grimly.

Eric looked to Enrico Gomez, vice president of operations. Enrico had recently joined PP Inc. Enrico cleared his throat and answered, "As you know, I started with PP exactly twenty-nine days ago and I apologize that I don't know all the details."

"Enrico has jumped into the business very quickly despite the fact that he is new to our team," Eric said encouragingly.

"We have two of the same products as VVP," Mike added.

"What are those products?" Ross asked.

"XLY004 and XYT003," answered Eric.

"Those are your most important products," Ross looked vaguely surprised.

"At the moment, yes," Eric confirmed. "But not after we have finished our new factories."

"You'll build a new factory behind this building," Jill said, trying to get a confirmation to her conjecture.

"Actually, we are building two separate factories. One behind this building and one seven miles from here."

"Why the seven-mile distance?" she asked.

"Our suppliers are in that area. The site is located next to our main supplier."

"Who is your main supplier?"

"XYC Inc.," Eric answered.

"Well, I'm not familiar with that company," Ross said, embarrassed.

"XYC will be our main supplier. We haven't yet purchased anything from XYC," Eric admitted.

"Have you known XYC for any length of time?" Jill asked, studying Eric. The other men appeared to be slightly bored. "We have heard that the company has a good reputation," Eric continued.

"Who said that?" Jill demanded.

"Our main owner," Eric said, lowering his voice.

"Will they use the same supplier?" Ross asked.

"They are currently using the supplier for their other products. XYC has a variety of products," Eric confirmed.

"Are all your suppliers here?" Jill requested.

"Yes, for the most part," Eric stated shortly.

"But I have differing information," Jill said as she opened the four-month-old, sixty-two-page prospectus for initial public offering. "You recently got your shares listed," she noted.

"Yes, we did," Eric confirmed cheerfully. All the other representatives of PP Inc. were smiling, too.

"The offering price was $12 and now the share is up to $17. The share price went up to $24, but two weeks ago, it came down again. That's when your difficulties with Malaysian supplier MaleX went public," Jill said. She looked from one to the other.

Enrico was shifting uncomfortably in his seat. Eric leaned forward as Kim Lane, vice president of marketing, leaned back in her comfortable, soft leather chair. Dexter shifted from right to left and left to right.

"There is no longer any problem with our Malaysian supplier. We have resolved it. We issued a press release about our Malaysian supplier some days ago," Mike explained in a determined voice.

"You had problems with the quality of your products?"

"Yes, we did. That was in the past and now we are looking ahead," declared Dexter.

"Your sales rose from $30 million last year to $50 million this year," Jill stated.

"Our sales are growing very fast. We are on target," Kim confirmed.

"At the same time, your inventory rose from $5 million to $15 million. Did you have problems with your inventory?" Jill questioned. Dexter turned hesitantly in his chair.

"Not exactly; we wanted to make extra inventory so that we could deliver more quickly to you."

"Thank you, that is nice of you, but did you have any obsolete inventory?"

"There was some raw material for an old model of the copy X computer, which we are no longer using. That was only a small part."

"How small?"

"A few million dollars." That was not very small, Jill thought to herself.

"Your accounts receivable were $4 million and accounts payable $5 million—a slight imbalance," Jill continued.

"We did have a good level of cash after the IPO. We didn't have any payment problems. There were some delays in payments to our Malaysian supplier due to their bad deliveries."

"Your operating loss amounted to $4 million and the net loss was $1 million," Jill said firmly and looked at the management team.

"According to our calculations, we'll turn a profit next year after our factory expansion," Dexter replied.

"After the expansion, you will need more working capital," Jill stated quickly.

"Yes, you are right," Dexter admitted. "Our bankers are supporting us in the short term. They have promised," Dexter continued.

"What is your main bank?" Jill asked, following her list.

"Chase Manhattan Bank," answered Dexter fluently.

"You reported in your IPO prospectus that you do not yet have the funding needed to build factory one. There is no mention of factory two," Jill questioned.

"That was four months ago. Our profitability is better than we expected. Our costs are down. Very good people are working for us. The situation has changed a lot," Dexter explained.

"How many employees do you have?"

"Forty."

"That isn't many."

"True, but we are growing very quickly. A year ago, we had only twenty employees," Eric agreed.

"Your company is young."

"Yes and we try hard. We want to be number one in our branch within three years."

"That is a very ambitious target."

"The branch is new and our technology is currently the leading in this field," Dexter pointed out. "We are profitable, we are growing, and we are sure we will find funding for the new factory," Dexter gestured openly with his hands and looked to his colleagues, who nodded.

"According to this prospectus, you are still $30 million short," Jill said, keeping her eyes on the prospectus.

"That was four months ago," Dexter said in a loud voice.

"How can you get that amount of currency in such a short time. Your building should be completed in two months' time," Jill said, looking directly at Dexter.

"That is true. We are on schedule according to our plans." The dark eyes of Dexter, the senior vice president of finance, were very powerful. He had previously worked at a bigger company but in a lower position. He was in his forties and hungry for money—just like the other management team members. They wanted to be millionaires, and they were trying hard. Jill could feel it.

They ended up visiting the new construction, which was built in compliance with the government's strict environmental standards. It would be a very efficient building. Enrico had the main responsibility of keeping the construction work on schedule, and he was doing a good job of it.

While Ross was driving Jill to the airport, he asked for her impression of the company.

"The general impression is that they are capable and they really try hard. There may come some difficulties with the suppliers because they are completely new. They may still encounter difficulties with the Malaysian supplier. I think that they have underestimated the problem. It may not be a major problem, but anyway . . ." Jill said thoughtfully.

"What will be the role of the main owner, the competitor?" Ross asked with concern and turned the car into the short-term car park at the airport.

"Maybe this company is just an investor. I think that they can find the funding. It is positive that the building is on schedule. Do you need more comments at the moment? I'll write the corporate analysis and send it also to you?" Jill asked, turning toward Ross.

"No, that was all," Ross looked back at her, tired.

"We'll see later, hopefully, and thanks for driving." Jill took her bags.

"Thank you, Jill. It was nice working with you. Thanks for your opinions," Ross smiled and waved to her.

"Thanks, Ross, likewise."

Jill flew back to rainy London. It was the first time the entire day that she really felt exhausted. She opened her laptop and started writing the corporate analysis.

The management team at PP Inc. had made its dream come true. They had a vision and strict plans, which they followed up with corrective actions. PP Inc. worked hard with Success Inc. and with several other companies. After three years the entire management team—Eric, Dexter, Kim, and Enrico—were successful and respected top executives. PP Inc. was a great supplier for Success Inc. for several years.

Case 7: A Risk Supplier

"Hi, please come in," said a good-looking athletic man in his thirties, with a wide smile on his tanned face.

Jill stepped in and he led her politely through the corridors to a large white room with pillars and paintings in heavy gold frames. The room matched the style of the corridor. Jill didn't know the style specifically. The building was old, but the renovation had restored all the original details.

Mike Vanne flashed his teeth in a wide lazy smile. He wore a white-collared shirt with a gray suit and black shoes. The polished shoes were made of soft leather. "I apologize that we couldn't meet last week, but I was vacationing in Bali," Mike talked smoothly. "I live in Monaco, actually," he revealed, leaning back in his leather chair. "Of course, my businesses take me all over the world. Especially when it is a question of mergers and acquisitions, a rather frequent event over recent years," he added. Jill noticed the white teeth and smile again.

"You have made eleven acquisitions during the past two years and you have grown over 500 percent. Is this correct?" Jill asked.

"Yes, you are right. We are growing fast. You have to grow fast in this business to be number one," answered Mike.

"Are you number one in this industry?" Jill interrogated, already knowing the response. "Not just yet, but we are aiming to be number one," Mike explained, biting into a cookie.

"Your chair is a very busy man," Jill started.

"You mean Ari Villa. He is also a famous politician and politics keep him busy," Mike stated.

"I read in the newspaper that he is no longer interested in your company; he said that he was invited to be the chairman, but that he doesn't actually know much of anything about your company," Jill replied.

"He is busy and takes part in our meetings when he can," Mike hesitated, looking to the wall at a large, old painting. The man in the painting was staring directly at them; he had been a powerful man in his time.

"How often has he taken part in board meetings during the past year?" Jill asked curiously.

Mike answered quickly, "I don't remember exactly." Mike studied the painting with interest.

"Roughly," Jill insisted.

"Once or twice, I think," Mark replied after a long silence.

"How many board meetings did you have last year?"

"Ten or so," Mike stated. Ten meetings and the chairman of the board was not present. Jill made her conclusion quietly, looking at her papers.

"The main reason I am here is because company X acquired company Y, which was our supplier," Jill stated.

"I apologize if I don't know all the details about company Y," Mike explained.

"I suppose you took part in the acquisition?" Jill inquired, slightly raising her voice.

Mike admitted by nodding, "Yes, I did, but our lawyers and our CFO know the details the best."

"You have a new CFO?" Jill interrogated.

"Sandra Chia is from China. She has an excellent resume. Sandra has worked for our company for three months," Mike stated proudly.

"I suppose that she was expected to take part in this meeting, too," Jill stated shortly.

"I apologize. Sandra is very busy with the funding for our newest acquisition: Acquire Inc. in the United States, a small software company. We issued a press release about that two weeks ago," Mike continued.

Jill knew the company. It was relatively small and had some litigation going on. According to analysts, the company was in bad shape financially.

"The company has great ideas and a lot of patents," Mike said proudly.

"Nevertheless, shall we go over the financial figures of company X and company Y, which is our supplier and among your newest acquisitions?" Jill asked.

"Sure," Mike replied, glancing at his stylish watch.

"Company X was established in 1997. You changed your fiscal year in 1998 and in 1999. What is the reason for these changes?" Jill asked, staring at Mike's tanned face.

"Our business changed. Previously our fiscal year ended in May, but that was quite impractical. We changed the fiscal year to be the calendar year," Mike explained with a blank face.

"I see. Who is the main owner of company X?" Jill asked.

"I am one of the biggest owners. As for the other owners, I can't say. Our company is publicly owned and the ownership is constantly changing," Mike explained.

"Do you own your company directly or through other companies?" Jill asked directly.

"Reliable Ltd Holding is the main owner," Mike responded fluently.

"Is Reliable Ltd Holding a British company?" Jill continued her questioning.

"It is registered in the Virgin Islands. I own the whole company through some other companies," Mike stated proudly with a smile.

"There must be a huge amount of administrative work since there are several companies and transactions among them," Jill wondered aloud.

"Not at all. I have good employees taking care of accounting. We have not found any difficulty in handling several companies," Mike smiled confidently.

"What is the reason for the complicated structure of your company?" Jill asked.

"Tax reasons. We want to minimize taxes. You may have read in the newspaper that I have had some dispute with the tax authorities, but this was in the past. I know that I am right," Mike pointed out confidently.

"What if you run into difficulties with the tax authorities in the future?" Jill inquired curiously.

"I don't think I will," Mike was convinced.

"Your new subsidiary, Y Ltd, is our supplier. Please tell me why the company incurred heavy losses during the past year." Jill was going straight to the point.

"Incompetent management. The previous management didn't take care of the company." Mike let Jill know all the details.

"What is the expected capital expenditure for the next year?" Jill continued.

"I can't answer that question directly without our CFO present. Sandra is familiar with the figures. I suppose that we'll get the company going on a new upward trend. Of course, we have to get rid of the loss-making parts of the company," Mike added.

"X Inc. had recently been involved in numerous lawsuits," Jill stated.

"I have not heard anything about litigation. That cannot be true. Where did you get that information?" Mike lost his good manners and suddenly became impatient.

Jill ignored the change in his mood and continued calmly: "I ran a credit report on company X. If you disagree with the information, please contact the credit information company," she answered.

"I'll definitely do that to stop all the misleading talk that is hurting our company," Mike raised his voice. He broke off and glanced at his stylish watch impatiently. "Oh—I have to catch a 5:30 plane to New York. Excuse me, but I have to leave for the airport." Mike stood up. Jill couldn't do anything but gather up her belongings. She still had some questions left.

"We'd be happy to give you all the information you need," Mike added, leading her urgently across the hall and through the corridors toward the elevator.

Jill gazed at a painting of sailboats adorning the wall. "A beautiful boat," she sighed politely.

"I have several boats; this one is in Portofino, Italy," Mike stopped in front of the large sailing boat. "It is a fifty-foot Jeanneau. My pride and joy, *Anna,* named after my daughter," Mike no longer seemed to be in a hurry. Jill focused on his lips, waiting for the white teeth to come shining through. He tried to conceal a smile, but it was impossible. He chuckled. "It's an incredible boat," he murmured. "Anyway, it's time to go." Jill shook Mike's warm hand and closed the big heavy door.

A year after Jill's visit, the dot-com boom was over. Mike's company was taken off NASDAQ because of allegations of accounting mistakes. Within two years, Mike was involved in several lawsuits concerning the misleading information he had given about the company. CFO Sandra Chia was released from all proceedings.

Success Inc. had to find another supplier; its supplier had lost its technical edge as a result of changes in key R&D personnel after the merger.

Part Three

Examples

Part Three

Examples

Using Analyzing Tools and Useful Templates

THIS CHAPTER ADDRESSES templates for the two types of analysis and the rating guidelines. As a so-called limited-scope examination, the short analysis may be the most effective use of company resources when only a quick check of the supplier's performance is needed. As a full-scope examination, the corporate analysis requires a review of every area of the company, rather than targeting specific areas.

You need to choose the correct company or companies to analyze. If the parent company owns your supplier 100 percent, you must analyze both the financial figures of the group and the parent company. If you obtain financial information from the subsidiary (your supplier), it supports your work. However, there is normally no sense in analyzing only the subsidiary, because the parent company may exert a strong influence on its financial figures.

6.1 Short Analysis—Financial Analysis

You can convert the short analysis template into an Excel template to calculate key ratios. A financial analysis provides you with a quick analysis of a company's financial performance. It is based on historical financial figures. The information provided cannot exceed the level of the original financial statements. (See Figures 6-1 and 6-2.)

Figure 6-1. Income statement.

FINANCIAL ANALYSIS

Name and address of the supplier
Company structure
(Does this supplier have a parent company?)
Ownership
Public company/private company

Income statement

Consolidated/nonconsolidated

Currency:

Accounting period:

Fiscal years

	2003	2002	2001
Net sales			
Cost of goods sold			
Gross profit			
Operating expenses:			
Total operating expenses			
Operating income			
Interest income			
Interest expense, net			
Other income (expense), net			
Provisions for income taxes			
Extraordinary charges			
Net income (loss)			

Summary

Summarize the findings of the key ratios at the end of Figure 6-2 on page 164. If the key ratios show a weak financial position and decreasing profitability, you need to consider whether a more comprehensive analysis of the supplier should be made.

Figure 6-2. Balance sheet and key ratios.

BALANCE SHEET

Consolidated/nonconsolidated

Currency:

Fiscal years

Accounting period

	2003	2002

BALANCE SHEET

ASSETS

Current assets:

Cash and cash equivalents		
Short-term investments		
Accounts receivable		
Inventories, net		
Deferred income taxes		
Other (e.g., prepaid expenses, tax receivables)		
Total current assets		

Property, plant, and equipment, net		
Goodwill and intangibles, net		
Long-term investments		
Other (e.g., long-term deposits)		
TOTAL ASSETS		

(continues)

6.2 Comprehensive Analysis—Corporate Analysis Template

Once a supplier is identified as the target of a comprehensive examination, a corporate analysis should focus on the combined impact of the environment in which the company operates, the company's financial and operating results, and the extent and effectiveness of the company's internal control.

A corporate analysis gives you the possibility to build a more

Figure 6-2. (continued)

LIABILITIES AND SHAREHOLDERS' EQUITY

Current liabilities:

Current portion of long-term debt

Accounts payable

Accrued (e.g., liabilities, payroll, other benefits)

Accrued payroll and related benefits

Income taxes payable

Total current liabilities

Long-term liabilities

Long-term debt, net of current portion

Deferred income tax liability

Other

Total long-term liabilities

Shareholders' equity

Stocks (e.g., common, preferred, treasury)

Additional paid-in capital

Accumulated other comprehensive (loss)

Retained earnings

Total shareholders' equity

TOTAL LIABILITIES AND SHAREHOLDERS' EQUITY

KEY RATIOS

	2003	2002
Revenue change, %		
Operating income, % of revenue		
Current ratio		
Debt-to-total assets ratio		

See the formulas of key ratios in Subchapter 4.5.

comprehensive picture of the company and the company group in which it belongs. (See Figure 6-3.)

Rating

The rating of a supplier's performance can be made using different methods, such as subjective rating, quantitative rating, and the supplier's self-assessment.

❑ A *subjective rating* is given by the analyst or purchasing manager, who analyzes the company. A subjective rating can be

Figure 6-3. Format of a corporate analysis of suppliers.

A	**EXECUTIVE SUMMARY**
	Recommendations
	Strengths, Weaknesses, Opportunities, and Threats (SWOT)
	Conclusions
	Risk rating

B	**ENVIRONMENT**
	Country
	Political environment
	Regulatory environment
	Market
	Customers
	Suppliers and logistics
	Competitors

C	**COMPANY**
	Strategy
	Company life cycle
	Technology
	Ownership
	Corporate structure
	—Holding company
	—Subsidiary
	Organization
	Management
	Acquisitions and mergers

D	**FINANCIAL ANALYSIS**
	Financial statements
	Key ratios
	Forecast

based on specified elements, which the analyst or purchasing manager values according to the relationship among the elements. The results in the subjective rating may differ if separate individuals are rating the company. A subjective rating is based on the expertise of the persons rating the company.

❏ A *quantitative rating* is based on measurable figures and ignores subjective opinions. However, quantitative rating is mechanical and cannot take into account the expert's opinion, which in some cases is vitally important for reaching optimal results.

❏ A *supplier's self-assessment* is made by the supplier itself. Obviously, it is highly subjective and points out the supplier's best aspects. The self-assessment can be characterized as sophisticated marketing of the supplier's products and services. The advantage is that self-assessments save costs when assessing suppliers.

Corporate Analysis

A corporate analysis is a subjective rating because of the relatively strong influence of the analyst's opinion. The rating of a corporate analysis has three categories, each with a plus or minus (for example, for the category *good* there would also be good+ and good−) giving a more detailed description of the company's position within the category. You can create more categories if necessary. The purpose is to keep the rating as simple and informative as possible. (See Figure 6-4.)

Financial Analysis

Financial analysis is a mechanical rating based on key ratios, leaving less room for subjective opinions. However, you need to remember that ratios do not tell you the whole story—you should know the background behind the figures. Financial analysis is a simple tool to provide quick answers by analyzing a supplier or comparing a supplier base. (See Figure 6-5.)

Figure 6-4.   Corporate analysis and rating.

Rating categories in corporate analysis

- **1. Good +/–**

  A company with profitable operations.

  Requirements: operating profit for past three years, debt/total assets ratio of 60% or less, current ratio of 1.5 or above, credit rating in good investment grade, excellent management, good owners, and stable history

- **2. Average +/–**

  A company with mainly profitable operations. The company may have had an operating loss a year or two ago.

  Requirements: operating profit in the newest annual income statement, debt/total assets ratio of 70% or less, current ratio of over 1, credit rating in investment grade, good management, good owners, relatively stable history.

- **3. Poor +/–**

  A company with unstable and/or unprofitable operations. Start-up companies belong to this group along with existing companies that incur an operating loss and have a weak financial position.

  Requirements: operating loss, debt/total assets ratio over 70%, current ratio of less than 1, credit rating under investment grade, several "warning flag" conditions.

Figure 6-5.   Financial analysis and rating.

Rating categories in financial analysis

	1. Good	2. Average	3. Poor
Operating profit from revenues for the year	Over 5%	Positive	Operating loss
Debt/total assets ratio	60% or less	70% or less	Over 70%
Current ratio	1.5 or over	Over 1	Less than 1
Credit rating	Good investment grade	Investment grade	Under investment grade

7

Studying Examples

7.1 Short Analysis

This chapter gives some basic examples of supplier analysis. First, a short analysis of Sanmina-SCI is presented. Following that, there are examples of more in-depth corporate analyses of Intel Corporation and Marconi PLC. The sources of the financial figures in these examples are the official company reports. The information was accurate at press time.

Example 1: Sanmina-SCI Corporation (U.S.)

Sanmina-SCI Corporation is a U.S.-based, publicly listed company. It is easy to find financial information about Sanmina-SCI Corporation from public sources.

The financial statements of the company, followed by the short analysis of the financial statements, are presented in Figures 7-1 through 7-4.

Summary

Revenue decreased by 4 percent during the previous year. The operating income remained at 2 percent of revenues. The financial condition remained strong because the current ratio and debt-to-total assets ratios were good.

7.2 Corporate Analysis

Examples of corporate analysis are presented in Examples 2 and 3 beginning on page 173. Example 2 is a normal length corporate analysis of Intel Corporation, a U.S.-based listed company. Example 3 is taken from Marconi PLC, a U.K.-based listed company. Example 3 includes comments to guide you in the analysis and to help you come to your own conclusions.

Figure 7-1. Sanmina-SCI consolidated statements of operations according to SEC filings.

Sanmina-SCI Corporation
Information according to SEC filings

Consolidated statements of operations in millions $	Sept. 29 2001	Sept. 30 2000	Oct. 02 1999
Net sales	4.054	4.239	2.621
Cost of sales	3.513	3.562	2.186
Gross profit	541	677	434
Operating expenses:			
Selling, general, and administrative	240	236	174
Amortization of goodwill and intangibles	26	24	16
Write-down of long-lived assets	40	9	11
Merger costs	13	20	6
Restructuring costs	159	27	30
Total operating expenses	478	316	237
Operating income	63	361	197
Interest income	73	43	16
Interest expense, net	−55	−47	−43
Other income (expense), net	2	1	−1
Income before provisions for income taxes	83	358	169
Provisions for income taxes	43	143	64
Income before extraordinary charge	40	215	105
Extraordinary charge	0	5	0
Net income (loss)	$40	$210	$105

Figure 7-2. Sanmina-SCI balance sheet according to SEC filings.

Consolidated Currency: US$ (in millions) Fiscal years ended: September	Sept. 29 2001	Sept. 30 2000

BALANCE SHEET

ASSETS

Current assets:

	Sept. 29 2001	Sept. 30 2000
Cash and cash equivalents	$567	$998
Short-term investments	821	265
Accounts receivable	410	715
Inventories, net	504	609
Deferred income taxes	160	87
Income taxes receivable	93	0
Prepaid expense and other	28	30
Total current assets	2583	2704
Property, plant, and equipment, net	633	701
Goodwill and intangibles, net	294	347
Long-term investments	99	56
Deposits and other	31	28
Total assets	**$3.64**	**$3.84**

LIABILITIES AND STOCKHOLDERS' EQUITY

Current liabilities:

	Sept. 29 2001	Sept. 30 2000
Current portion of long-term debt	$16	$17
Accounts payable	332	541
Accrued liabilities	98	130
Accrued payroll and related benefits	46	54
Income taxes payable	0	48
Total current liabilities	492	790

Long-term liabilities

	Sept. 29 2001	Sept. 30 2000
Long-term debt, net of current portion	1.219	1.201
Deferred income tax liability	61	62
Other	27	24
Total long-term liabilities	1.307	1.287

Stockholders' equity

	Sept. 29 2001	Sept. 30 2000
Preferred stock	0	0
Common stock	3	3
Treasury stock	−46	0
Additional paid-in capital	1.267	1.169
Accumulated other comprehensive (loss)	−14	−9
Retained earnings	631	596
Total stockholders' equity	1.841	1.759
Total liabilities and shareholders' equity	**$3.64**	**$3.84**

Figure 7-3. Sanmina-SCI financial analysis/income statement.

FINANCIAL ANALYSIS

Sanmina-SCI	2700 North First Street, San Jose, California 95131, U.S.
Company structure:	parent company; consolidated financial statements
Public company:	listed in NASDAQ
Ownership:	

Consolidated income statement
Currency: $ in millions
Fiscal years ended: September

	Sept. 29 2001	Sept. 30 2000	Oct. 02 1999

Consolidated statements of operations

	Sept. 29 2001	Sept. 30 2000	Oct. 02 1999
Net sales	4,054	4,239	2,621
Cost of sales	3.513	3.562	2.186
Gross profit	541	677	434
Operating expenses:			
Total operating expenses	478	316	237
Operating income	63	361	197
Interest income	73	43	16
Interest expense, net	−55	−47	−43
Other income (expense), net	2	1	−1
Provisions for income taxes	43	143	64
Extraordinary charges	0	5	0
Net income (loss)	$40	$211	$105

Figure 7-4. Sanmina-SCI financial analysis/balance sheet and key ratios.

BALANCE SHEET
Consolidated
Currency: US$ (in millions)
Fiscal years ended: September

	Sept. 29 2001	Sept. 30 2000
BALANCE SHEET		
ASSETS		
Current assets:		
Cash and cash equivalents and short-term investments	$1,389	$1,263
Accounts receivable	410	715
Inventories, net	504	609
Deferred income taxes	160	87
Other (e.g., prepaid expenses, tax receivable)	121	30
Total current assets	2,583	2,704
Property, plant, and equipment, net	633	701
Goodwill and intangibles, net	294	347
Long-term investments	99	56
Other (e.g., long-term deposits)	31	28
Total assets	$3.640	$3.836
LIABILITIES AND STOCKHOLDERS' EQUITY		
Current liabilities:		
Current portion of long-term debt	16	17
Accounts payable	332	541
Accrued (e.g., liabilities, payroll, other benefits)	144	184
Income taxes payable	0	48
Total current liabilities	492	790
Long-term liabilities		
Long-term debt, net of current portion	1.219	1.201
Other (all other long-term liabilities)	88	86
Total long-term liabilities	1,307	1,287
Stockholders' equity		
Stocks (e.g., common, preferred, treasury)	−43	3
Additional paid-in capital	1.267	1.169
Accumulated other comprehensive (loss)	−14	−9
Retained earnings	631	596
Total stockholders' equity	1.841	1.759
Total liabilities and shareholders' equity	3,640	3,836

(*continues*)

Figure 7-4. (continued)
KEY RATIOS

	2001	2000	Year 2001
Revenue change, %	–4%	62%	Poor
Operating income, % from revenues	2%	9%	Average
Current ratio	5.25	3.42	Good
Debt-to-total assets ratio	49%	54%	Good
Total rating			**Good**

Example 2: Intel Corporation (U.S.)

Headquarters: 2200 Mission College Boulevard, Santa Clara, California 95952-8119

Web site: http://www.intel.com

Executive Summary
Recommendations

The remarks in italics show the possible general assumptions at that point.

The recommendation you give depends on the type and scale of business you are going to engage in with this company.

Conclusion

In 2001 Intel's financial condition remained very strong, even though the company suffered a downturn market with decreasing margins. Intel is a company with a long, stable history.

Strengths

Credit rating: October 9, 2002, by Standard & Poor's

LT Foreign Issuer Credit: A +

LT Local Issuer Credit: A +

ST Foreign Issuer Credit: A-1 +

ST Local Issuer Credit: A-1 +

Intel had good credit ratings in investment grade.

Weaknesses

❑ Decreasing revenues and increasing cost of sales and cost of operations.

Opportunities

Intel is still financially strong compared with other companies in the semiconductor sector. The company has the opportunity to keep a leadership position in a difficult market.

Threats

Threats include possible strong price pressure.

Intel Corporation

Risk rating 1   Good company

Environment

Country

❏ *Political and regulatory environment.* Intel Corporation (called Intel) has headquarters in a politically stable country. The majority of Intel's wafers, microprocessors, and chipsets were manufactured within the United States at facilities in New Mexico, Arizona, Oregon, Colorado, California, and Massachusetts. However, at least a significant portion of the wafer manufacturing was conducted at facilities in Israel and Ireland. The country risk rating in Israel is as follows: Moody's, A2; Standard & Poor's, A −; and Fitch, A −. In comparison, the country risk ratings in the United Kingdom and United States are as follows: Moody's, Aaa; Standard & Poor's, AAA; and Fitch, AAA. Israel has a higher country risk compared to the United States and United Kingdom (country rating in the fall of 2002). (See Appendix, App.3 Credit-Rating Agencies.)

Market

❏ *Customers.* Major customers are in the following industries: original equipment manufacturers, who make computer systems, cellular handsets, and handheld computing devices, telecommunications and networking communications equipment, and peripherals; PC and network communications product users, who buy Intel's PC Enhancements, networking products, and business communications products through retailers; other manufacturers, including makers of a wide range of industrial and communications equipment.

Intel has a diversified customer base, which means that Intel is not dependent on only one sector of business. Intel primarily delivers standard products.

❑ *Suppliers and logistics.* The information from suppliers and logistics is mainly only available directly from the company.

❑ *Competitors.* Many of Intel's competitors have licensed their patents, which means a license fee for Intel. However, Intel's competitors can design products that compete with Intel products.

Company

Intel is a semiconductor chip maker with common stock traded on the NASDAQ Stock Market under the symbol INTC and on the Swiss Exchange.

Strategy

According to the current corporate strategy, Intel is a semiconductor chip maker, whose products include microprocessors, chipsets, boards, networking, and communication products.

If this company is your strategic partner, is its current and possible future corporate strategy in line with your corporate strategy?

Is the strategy of the business unit, which is your supplier, in line with your current and future purchasing strategy?

Corporate Structure

Intel Corporation and its subsidiaries:
Intel has a clear company structure.

Organizational Structure

Intel has four operating segments according to the various product lines: the Intel Architecture business, the Intel Communications Group, the Wireless Communications and Computing Group, and the New Business Group. Intel reported only three segments for 2001.

Divisions

Intel Architecture Business includes the following segments: microprocessors; desktop platform, mobile platform, server and workstation platforms; chipset; board-level products; and e-business solutions.

Intel Communications Group includes the subgroups Ethernet connectivity products, optical components, network processing components, and embedded control chips.

Wireless Communications and Computing Group contains segments such as flash memory, processors for handheld computing devices, and cellular baseband chipset.

Key Persons

Craig R. Barrett	Chief executive officer, a director of Intel since 1992
Andrew S. Grove	Chairman of the board, a director of Intel since 1974
Paul S. Otellini	President and chief operating officer, with Intel since 1994
Leslie L. Vadasz	Executive vice president and president, Intel Capital, a director of Intel since 1988
Andy D. Bryant	Executive vice president and chief financial and Enterprise Services officer, with Intel since 1994
Sean M. Maloney	Executive vice president and general manager, Intel Communications Group, with Intel since 1995
Michael R. Splinter	Executive vice president and general manager, Sales and Marketing Group, with Intel since 1996

Management has long experience in this type of business.

Head Count

As of December 29, 2001, Intel employed approximately 83,400 people worldwide.

Ownership

Classification of shareholders	Percentage of issued capital
Publicly owned company	

Financial Analysis

Intel has a well-known auditor: Ernst & Young LLP. (See Intel's consolidated balance sheet in Figure 7-5).

Current Assets

Cash and cash equivalents increased significantly from 2000 to 2001, but at the same time, short-term investments decreased. Short-term

Figure 7-5. Intel consolidated balance sheet assets.

Intel Corporation

CONSOLIDATED BALANCE SHEET

(US$, in millions)	Dec. 29, 2001	Dec. 30, 2000
ASSETS		
Current assets		
Cash and cash equivalents	$7,970	$2,976
Short-term investments	2,356	10,497
Trading assets	1,224	350
Accounts receivable, net allowance for		
doubtful accounts of 68 million (84 million in 2000)	2,607	4,129
Inventories	2,253	2,241
Deferred tax assets	958	721
Other current assets	265	236
Total current assets	**17,633**	**21,150**
Property, plant, and equipment:		
Land and buildings	10,709	7,416
Machinery and equipment	21,605	15,994
Construction in progress	2,042	4,843
	34,356	28,253
Less accumulated depreciation	16,235	13,240
Property, plant, and equipment, net	**18,121**	**15,013**
Marketable strategic equity securities	155	1,915
Other long-term investments	1,319	1,797
Goodwill, net	4,330	4,977
Acquisition-related intangibles, net	797	964
Other assets	2,040	2,129
TOTAL ASSETS	**$44,395**	**$47,945**

investments were converted into cash. Accounts receivable decreased to $2,607 million from $4,129 million in 2001. Inventories were almost at the same level in both of those fiscal years.

Property, Plant, and Equipment, Net

Land, buildings, machinery, and equipment increased from 2000 to 2001.

Other Items in Assets

All the other items did not change significantly. Net goodwill was $4,330 million in 2001. (See Figure 7-6.)

Figure 7-6. Intel consolidated balance sheet liabilities and shareholders' equity.

LIABILITIES AND SHAREHOLDERS' EQUITY

in millions $	Dec. 29, 2001	Dec. 30, 2000
Current liabilities		
Short-term debt	409	378
Accounts payable	1,769	2,387
Accrued compensation and benefits	1,179	1,696
Accrued advertising	560	782
Deferred income on shipments to distributors	418	674
Other accrued liabilities	1,247	1,440
Income taxes payable	988	1,293
Total current liabilities	**6,570**	**8,650**
Long-term debt	**1,050**	**707**
Deferred tax liabilities	945	1,266
Commitments and contingencies		
Shareholders' equity:		
Preferred stock, $0.001 par value, 50 shares		
Authorized; none issued		
Common stock, $0.01 par value, 10,000 shares		
Authorized; 6,690 issued and outstanding (6,721 in 2000) and		
capital in excess of par value	8,833	8,486
Acquisition-related unearned stock		
Compensation	–178	–97
Accumulated other comprehensive income	25	195
Retained earnings	27,150	28,738
Total shareholders' equity	**35,830**	**37,322**
TOTAL LIABILITIES AND SHAREHOLDERS' EQUITY	**$44,395**	**$47,945**

Current Liabilities

Current liabilities on the whole decreased from $8,650 million in 2000 to $6,570 million in 2001. Long-term debt increased from $707 million in 2000 to $1,050 million in 2001. Total shareholders' equity decreased to $35,830 million. However, total assets decreased to $44,390 million; therefore, shareholders' equity was relatively the same level in the previous year period. (See Figure 7-7.)

Revenues

Revenues decreased 21 percent, from $33,726 million in the previous year period to $26,539 million. However, at the same time, the cost of goods sold increased 7 percent, from $12,650 million to $13,487 million, and operating costs and expenses increased 4 percent, from $23,331 million to $24,283 million. Because of significant increases in costs, operating income dropped 78 percent, from $10,395 million to $2,256 million. Net income remained positive even though the decrease was substantial. (See Figure 7-8.)

Figure 7-7. Intel consolidated statements of income.

Intel Corporation

CONSOLIDATED STATEMENTS OF INCOME

(US$, millions)	Fiscal year ended December 29, 2001		
	2001	2000	1999
Net revenues	$26,539	$33,726	$29,389
Cost of goods sold	13,487	12,650	11,836
Research and development	3,796	3,897	3,111
Marketing, general and administrative	4,464	5,089	3,872
Amortization of goodwill and other acquisition-related intangibles and costs	2,338	1,586	411
Purchased in-process research and development	198	109	392
Operating costs and expenses	24,283	23,331	19,622
Operating income	2,256	10,395	9,767
Gains (losses) on equity securities, net	−466	3,759	883
Interest and other, net	393	987	578
Income before taxes	2,183	15,141	11,228
Provisions for taxes	892	4,606	3,914
Net income	$1,291	$10,535	$7,314

Figure 7-8. Intel consolidated statements and cash flow.

Intel Corporation

CONSOLIDATED STATEMENTS AND CASH FLOW

(US$, millions)	Fiscal year ended December 29, 2001		
	2001	2000	1999
Cash and cash equivalents, beginning of year	$2,976	$3,695	$2,038
Net cash provided by **operating activities**	8,654	12,827	12,134
Net cash used for **investing activities**	–195	–10035	–6249
Net cash used for **financing activities**	–3465	–3511	4,228
Net increase (decrease) in cash and cash equivalents	4,995	–719	1,657
Cash and cash equivalents, end of year	$7,970	$2,976	$3,695

Consolidated statements and cash flows are shortened from the original consolidated statements and cash flows presented by Intel. Net cash provided by operating activities was $8,654 million in 2001.

Legal Proceedings

Legal proceedings are reported in SEC Form 10-F.

Research and Development

Intel states that it maintains its competitive position because of its emphasis on research and development. The R&D centers are located mainly in the United States, but also in other locations such as Israel, Malaysia, India, China, and Russia. Research and development costs were $3,796 million, or 14 percent from net revenues in 2001. (See Figure 7-9.)

Figure 7-9. Key ratios—Intel.

KEY RATIOS

	Fiscal year ended December 29, 2001			
	2001	2000	1999	Year 2001
Revenues change, %	–21%	15%		Poor
Operating income, % of revenue	9%	31%	33%	Good
Current ratio	2.68	2.45		Good
Debt-to-total assets ratio	19%	22%		Good
Total rating				Good

Forecast: Future

Intel has a strong background and good possibilities to be profitable in the future.

Subsidiaries

Selected Acquisitions

During 2001, Intel acquired eleven businesses. The following were among the companies acquired: Xircom, VxTel, LightLogic, and Cognet.

Several 100 percent–owned subsidiaries worldwide.

Sources of Information

SEC filings: Form 10-F Intel Corporation, for the fiscal year that ended December 29, 2001.

Web site: www.intel.com

Example 3: Marconi PLC (U.K.)

The remarks in italics show the possible general assumptions at that point.

Headquarters: 1 Bruton Street, London WIJ 6AQ, United Kingdom
Web site: http://www.marconi.com

Executive Summary

Recommendations

The recommendation you give depends on the type and scale of the business you are going to engage in with the company.

Conclusions

Please note the several warning flags, changes, or conditions that you can find from Marconi PLC. (See Subchapter 1.2.)

❑ Change in core business: Marconi PLC changed its core business from defense electronics operations to communications in 1999 by selling the defense business Marconi Electronic Systems. Noncore activities were transferred to Marconi's capital group.

The risk to fail is higher with a new business than it is with an existing business. A new core business may give advantages in the future.

❑ Changes in management and other key personnel: resignation of several key persons.

Significant changes in management are symptoms of difficulties. The new management may help a company in achieving objectives.

❑ Significant selling of assets: Asset selling by consolidating facilities and properties.

In conjunction with losses, significant selling of assets shows that a company is trying to solve its financial problems by downsizing. A slimmer organization may give advantages in the future.

❑ Changes in accounting policy: Marconi changed three accounting policies since the last annual report in 2001. In the SEC Form 20-F, the consolidated financial statements were presented according to U.S. GAAP in 2000 and 2001. Marconi also restated accounts, which changed, for example, the reported revenues (turnover) for 2001.

It is difficult or even impossible to compare and analyze the real profitability of a company that is changing its accounting policies.

❑ Changes in organizational structure: Shaping the organization by outsourcing manufacturing operations, and back office infrastructure and other organizational changes by integrating the company's headquarters and divisional structure into a single organization.

In the short term, significant organizational changes may cause organizational problems and an inability to serve customers if the personnel are focused on internal change. In the long term, the new organization can give advantages to the company.

❑ Changes in credit ratings; agencies such as Standard & Poor's and Moody's downgraded Marconi's credit ratings from BB (less vulnerable to nonpayment than other speculative issues) and Ba1 on March 2001 to CC (highly vulnerable to nonpayment) and Caa3 in September 2002.

When credit ratings are downgraded, cost of capital increase. The increase in interest expenses means more costs on the income statement. (See Appendix.)

❑ Radical changes in the market: Trading conditions deteriorated throughout the year. The industry was affected by the rapid turnaround in demand for telecom equipment in 2001.

It is difficult to be profitable in a rapidly deteriorating market.

❑ Core R&D costs increased by 5 percent in 2002 compared with the 2001 fiscal year.

High R&D spending may only be a cost, but it is also an opportunity and investment in the future.

Other Comments

The largest division in the core business, Network Equipment, made the highest net sales, £1,762 million in the 2001 to 2002 period, and the biggest loss, £461 million; that is, the main core business incurred losses. A core business that is incurring losses is a negative sign.

In September 2001, Marconi was removed from FTSE 100 index, which includes the 100 largest companies in the United Kingdom based on market capitalization. It is bad for a company's reputation to be removed from a well-known index.

The restructuring is continuing: The company has announced further downsizing, asset selling, changing of corporate structure, and complete relisting of shares. After the complex financial structuring of the group, with bondholders and banks exchanging debt for equity, the financial structure of Marconi will be healthier.

These measures show that the company is under heavy restructuring.

Risk Rating 3—Poor

Because of its weak financial condition, Marconi belongs to the high-risk category.

Environment
Country

Political and Regulatory Environment

Marconi PLC is a global telecommunications equipment and solutions company headquartered in London. There is no special political risk related to the United Kingdom. The country rating to the United Kingdom is AAA (highest rating in Standard & Poor's).

It is recommended that political risk be taken into account especially if your supplier has only one factory that produces for you and the factory is located in a politically unstable country.

Market and Customers

Marconi Group
The U.S. GAAP-based sales to British Telecom were £853 million and 15.5 percent from total sales in the fiscal year ending March 31, 2001. The following well-known companies were among Marconi's customers: AT&T, BellSouth, Cable & Wireless, Deutsche Telecom, France Telecom, Level 3 Communications, MCI WorldCom, Qwest, SBC Sprint, and Telecom Italia.

The list of customers includes leading telecom operators. The customer base is well diversified. However, if a company has only some customers and if those customers are in financial difficulties, the company may also face difficulties. SEC Form-20 shows customers per segment. *You can choose to study the segment of business in which you are interested.*

Suppliers and Logistics

The information about suppliers and logistics is usually only available directly from the company.

Competitors

Communications networks business operations are highly competitive. The most frequently mentioned competitors are as follows:

> *Public networks:* Alcatel, Cisco Systems, Ericsson, Lucent Technologies, Nortel, and Siemens

> *Private networks:* Cabletron, Cisco Systems, Lucent Technologies, and Nortel

The competition in different sectors is mentioned in SEC Form 20-F. A company may have global and local competitors.

Company

Marconi is a public company and its shares were listed on the London Stock Exchange and NASDAQ under the symbol (MONI) until July

5, 2002, when the company's listing changed from NASDAQ to OTC Bulletin Board.

Strategy

According to the current corporate strategy, Marconi is a global tele-communications equipment and solutions provider. The core business of network equipment incurred losses in the fiscal year ending March 31, 2002.

> *If this company is your strategic partner, is its current and possible future corporate strategy in alignment with your corporate strategy?*
>
> *Is the strategy of the business unit that is your supplier in alignment with your current and future purchasing strategy?*

Corporate Structure

Marconi PLC and Marconi Corporation PLC are incorporated as public limited companies under the laws of England and Wales. Marconi Corporation PLC is an indirect, wholly owned subsidiary of Marconi PLC.

Source: Form-20F, p. 1
Legal structure at March 31, 2001:

Marconi PLC (U.K.)	Parent company
Marconi Corporation PLC (U.K.)	100 percent–owned subsidiary of Marconi PLC

(Please see Marconi appendixes below)
Marconi has a clear company structure.

Organizational Structure

The telecom sector in general has been experiencing a downturn in 2001 and 2002. There have been several changes in the divisional structure in a relatively short period of time.

Changes in Divisional Structure

1. Before March 31, 2001, Marconi had five divisions: communications networks, communications services, mobile communications, data systems, and other.

2. From March 31, 2001, to September 4, 2001, Marconi was organized around three divisions: networks, wireless, and enterprise.

3. Effective September 4, 2001, the corporate structure was organized into two divisions: core communication businesses and a capital division. (See Figure 7-10.)

Management

Key Persons

D.C. Bonham	Chairman
Executive directors	
M. W. J. Parton	Chief Executive Officer
M. J. Donovan	Chief Operating Officer
S. Hare	Chief Financial Officer

Source: SEC Form 20-F and Annual report/Accounts, 2001/2002

In 2001, the following key personnel resigned:

On September 4, 2001, the resignations of Sir Roger Hurn and Lord Simpson from their positions on the board of directors and in the group were announced.

On April 10, 2001, John Mayo was appointed deputy chief executive of Marconi PLC. He resigned from all positions he held in the Marconi Group on July 6, 2001.

Figure 7-10. Marconi—divisions.

The core business is divided into three divisions:

£m	2001/2002	
	Sales	Operating (loss)/profit
Network Equipment	1,762	−461
Network Services	969	35
Mobile	369	−6

During the second half of the fiscal year 2001/2002, the chief human resources officer, R. I. Meakin, resigned from the board and the company.

There have been significant changes in top management.

Ownership

As of September 24, 2001, all directors and executive officers of Marconi PLC as a group owned 836,556 shares, which represented 0.03 percent of shares owned. The shares had different voting rights.

The ownership of the executive officers in Marconi was low. In companies where the executives have high ownership, their involvement—and therefore their personal interest in the success of the company—is higher. (See Figure 7-11.)

Banks and nominees are the main owners of Marconi. Therefore, the banks are interested in the results of their investment in the company.

The ownership of publicly owned companies is changing all the time, but the company possibly has the same main owners. It is important to know how willing the main owners are to finance the company if it needs fresh equity financing.

Head Count

Marconi was expecting to reduce the head count in its core business to around twenty-nine thousand by March 2002 from the 39,000 employed around March 31, 2001. According to the company, it expected to incur costs of around £450 million in relation to head count reductions and other associated restructuring charges during the fi-

Figure 7-11. Marconi—ownership.

Classification of shareholders	Percentage of issued capital
Banks/Nominees	70.9
Other Companies	8.5
Insurance Companies	0.3
Investment Trusts	0.1
Pension Funds	0
Individuals	20.2
Total	100

nancial year 2002. The company was told to integrate its current headquarters and three-divisional structure into a single organization, and to also outsource more operations, in particular parts of its back office structure.

Reductions in personnel mean costs in the short term. It also may mean loss of good personnel. After reductions, the cost structure is lighter and the company can generate savings in the future. The costs incurred by reducing personnel and closing factories are called *restructuring costs* on the income statement.

Financial Analysis

Marconi has a well-known auditor: Deloitte & Touche Chartered Accountants and Registered Auditors, London.

> *Is the auditor a well-known company or a private person?*
>
> *If the auditor is a private person, does the person have the competence to audit the financial statements?* (See Subchapter 4.1.)

Since Marconi is a U.K. company, it produces its U.K. annual financial statements under U.K. GAAP. The consolidated financial statements are prepared in accordance with U.S. GAAP.

Marconi changed three accounting policies since the last annual report in 2001. These consolidated financial statements are reported in SEC Form-20F filing for the fiscal year ending March 2001. (See Figure 7-12.)

Current Assets

Cash and cash equivalents decreased from 2000 to 2001. However, restricted cash existed in 2001, which brings the total amount of cash up to approximately the same level as in 2000. Marketable securities increased from £178 million in 2000 to £469 million in 2001. Marketable securities are also possible to convert quickly to cash.

It is important to monitor if the cash is decreasing significantly in a company that is generating losses. Most companies that go bankrupt are profitable, but they run out of short-term cash to deal with trade creditors, particularly when expanding. You should also find out how willing the owners are to invest in the company.

Figure 7-12. Marconi consolidated balance sheet, assets.
Marconi plc and subsidiaries

CONSOLIDATED BALANCE SHEET

(In millions £)

	Mar. 31, 2000	Mar. 31, 2001
ASSETS		
Current assets		
Cash and cash equivalents	544	373
Restricted cash	—	132
Marketable securities	178	469
Accounts receivable, net of allowance for doubtful accounts	1,483	1,799
Inventories	815	1,582
Prepaid expenses and other current assets	236	240
Deferred income taxes	133	239
Net assets of discontinued operations	408	490
Total current assets	**3,797**	**5,324**
Property, plant, and equipment, net	681	1,052
Marketable securities	14	6
Investments in affiliates	569	120
Goodwill and other intangibles, net	4,699	5,449
Other noncurrent assets	95	159
TOTAL ASSETS	**9,855**	**12,110**

Accounts receivable was high and even increased from 2000 to 2001.

Inventories increased significantly from £815 million in 2000 to £1,582 million in 2001. All items in the inventory increased: finished goods, work-in-process, and raw materials.

Inventory can increase because of a market slowdown or as a natural result of sales increases. Both of these facts were significant in the Marconi case.

There were no significant changes in prepaid expenses and other current assets, deferred income taxes, and net assets of discontinued operations.

Property, Plant, and Equipment, Net

Property and plant and equipment in particular increased from £681 million to £1,052 million. *If property and plant and equipment are decreasing significantly while a company is generating losses, the company is selling assets to survive.*

Marketable Securities

The amount of long-term marketable securities was low.

Investments in Affiliates

Investments in affiliates decreased significantly from £569 million in 2000 to £120 million in 2001.

Goodwill and Other Intangibles, Net

This item increased from £4,699 million in 2000 to £5,449 million in 2001. The increase in goodwill was related to several acquisitions Marconi made in 2000 and 2001.

If goodwill is high and the market on a downward trend, a company has to take a write-down of goodwill, which increases costs on the income statement. An increasing cost burden may mean a net loss on the income statement. A net loss decreases shareholders' equity. If shareholders' equity decreases to negative, bankruptcy is more likely. (See Subchapter 1.2 for warning flags.)

Other Noncurrent Assets

The amount of other noncurrent assets was relatively low. (See Figure 7-13.)

Current Liabilities

Short-Term Borrowings

Short-term borrowings decreased from £1,821 million to £1,408 million in 2001.

If a company is heavily indebted and short-term borrowings increase significantly, it may mean that the company can no longer obtain long-term

Figure 7-13. Marconi consolidated balance sheet, liabilities, and shareholders' equity.

LIABILITIES AND SHAREHOLDERS' EQUITY

	Mar. 31, 2000	Mar. 31, 2001
Current liabilities		
Short-term borrowings	1,821	1,408
Current maturities of long-term debt	9	47
Accounts payable	742	875
Accrued expenses and other current liabilities	1,477	1,599
Deferred income taxes	45	146
Total current liabilities	4,094	4,075
Long-term debt	938	2,269
Deferred income taxes	619	594
Other liabilities	149	170
Equity forward contracts	—	215
Minority interests	16	15
Shareholders' equity		
Treasury stock	—	–8
Ordinary shares	136	139
Additional paid-in capital	486	815
Retained earnings	3,577	3,611
Accumulated other comprehensive (loss)/income	–160	215
Total shareholders' equity	4,039	4,772
TOTAL LIABILITIES AND SHAREHOLDERS' EQUITY	9,855	12,110

financing. The negative aspect about short-term financing is the quick repayment requirement, which requires cash. The repayment may cause difficulties in heavily indebted companies.

Current Maturity of Long-Term Debt

Only some long-term debts matured within a year.

Refinancing may be a problem if a company is heavily indebted and the long-term debt will mature within a year.

Accounts Payable

Accounts payable increased from £742 million to £875 million.

If accounts payable are increasing while accounts receivable are decreasing, it is likely that a company is facing short-term financial difficulties.

Accrued Expenses and Other Current Liabilities

This item increased from £1,477 million to £1,599 million in 2001.

The contents of other items are always good to know. Other costs may include internal liabilities in the company group.

Deferred Income Taxes

This is a normal item to pay in the future.

Long-Term Debt

Indebtedness increased while long-term debt increased from £938 million in 2000 to £2,269 million in 2001.

Other Liabilities

Marconi PLC's other liabilities were low.

You should know the contents of other liabilities if they are high.

Equity Forward Contracts

This item does not normally exist in balance sheets.

Minority Interest

This is a normally low amount if it exists in the balance sheet.

Shareholders' Equity

Total shareholders' equity increased from £4,039 million in 2000 to £4,772 million in 2001. In 2001, because of the share and option plans, additional paid-in capital increased from £486 million in 2000 to £815 million in 2001. (See Figure 7-14.)

Shareholders' equity increases through additional paid-in capital and retained earnings. In a nutshell, Marconi got more property, plant and equipment, goodwill, and other intangibles, which it paid for mainly by taking on long-term debts.

Revenues

Revenues rose 24 percent from £4,427 million to £5,491 million in the previous year.

Generally, note the direction of the net sales.

Figure 7-14. Marconi consolidated statements of income.

Marconi plc and subsidiaries

CONSOLIDATED STATEMENTS OF INCOME

(In millions £)	Fiscal year ended March 31, 2000	2001
Revenues	4,427	5,491
Direct costs	2,750	3,366
Gross profit	1,677	2,125
Operating expenses		
Selling, general, and administrative	890	919
Research and development	341	566
Amortization of goodwill and other intangibles	487	660
Purchased in-process research and development	277	32
Gain on sale of businesses	0	–45
Total operating expenses	1,995	2,132
Operating income/(loss)	–318	–7
Other income/(expense)		
Gain on sale of investments	4	461
Equity in net income/(loss) of affiliates	83	–137
Interest income	102	46
Interest expense	–210	–199
Income/(loss) from continuing operations before income taxes and minority interests	–339	164
Income tax provision	–70	–44
Minority interests	–3	–5
Income/(loss) from continuing operations	–412	115
Discontinued operations		
Income from discontinued operations, net of income tax	22	45
Gain on discontinued operations, net of income tax	675	20
Net income	285	180

Direct Costs

Direct costs were £3,366 million in 2001, an increase of 22 percent from 2000. This increase was in line with the increase in revenues.

If direct costs are increasing and revenues are decreasing, a company needs restructuring.

Operating Expenses

Selling, general, and administrative expenses increased slightly from £890 million in 2000 to £919 million in 2001.

Pay attention if selling, general, and administrative costs are increasing relatively at the same time that revenues are increasing. If so, a company needs restructuring.

Research and Development

Research and development expenditure for the year increased in absolute terms to £566 million from £341 million a year earlier. As a proportion of revenues, R&D costs were 10 percent, compared with 8 percent the previous year.

If R&D costs are low, only some percentage of revenues, the company may only develop some new products.

Amortization of goodwill and other intangibles was £660 million.

A high amount of amortization decreases the net result.

Purchased in-process R&D was low.

Not normally a significant item.

Gain on sale of businesses: Marconi incurred some losses by selling businesses.

In some cases, a company may incur losses in operations but gains on the sale of business.

———

Total operating expenses were £2,132 million, that is, 39 percent of revenues in 2001.

A company needs to downsize if the total operating expenses are substantial compared to revenues.

Operating Income

Operating income (loss) amounted to £7 million during 2001. This decline was driven by the substantial increase in total operating expenses caused by significant amortization of goodwill and other intangibles and increased R&D costs.

Operating profit or loss is a significant item to look at in the income statement. The reasons behind the operating loss or profit must be determined.

Other income/(expense), which includes gains on the sale of investments, equity in net income/(loss) of affiliates, income interest, and interest expense, totaled £171 million in 2001. Marconi gained income by selling off investments.

Pay attention if a company has high interest expenses. A company needs good profitability to pay high interests. Unfortunately, the combination of high indebtedness and unprofitability is most common, and these are negative signs of the continuity of business.

Income/Loss from Continuing Operations

Income/(loss) from continuing operations before income taxes and minority interests was £115 million in 2001.

The income from continuing operations is naturally very essential. Discontinued operations are those that will not affect future business.

Net Income

Net income decreased 37 percent from £285 million to £180 million in the previous year.

Net income or loss is very significant, because net income increases and net loss decreases shareholders' equity in the balance sheet. Shareholders' equity is important for a company's financial strength. (See Figure 7-15.)

In 2001, net cash flow provided by operating activities of continuing operations was £541 million. Net cash (used for)/provided by operating activities of continuing operations was £541 million in 2001.

Figure 7-15. Marconi consolidated statements and cash flows.
Marconi plc and subsidiaries

CONSOLIDATED STATEMENTS OF CASH FLOWS

(In £ millions)	Fiscal year ended March 31,	
	2000	2001
Cash flow from operating activities:		
Net cash (used for)/provided by operating activities of continuing operations	403	−541
Cash flows from investing activities:		
Net cash provided by/(used for) investing activities	−2,973	−109
Cash flow from financing activities:		
Net cash provided by financing activities	1,644	431
Cash and cash equivalents, end of year	544	373

If operating cash flow is negative, a company cannot finance its opera-tions through cash flows. It is normal that start-up companies have an insuf-ficient cash flow from operating activities. Companies with a longer history in the market should be able to have positive cash flows from operation at least within a few years. In this case, operating cash flow was negative but overall cash flow was positive.

Marconi reported in its annual report and accounts for 2001 to 2002 that the order backlog in the core business fell from approxi-mately £2,100 million in March 2001 to approximately £1,700 mil-lion by March 2002. (See Figure 7-16.)

The lower level of orders reflects the difficult market conditions.

Lower order backlog means lower revenues and downsizing.

R&D expenses increased, mainly as a result of product launch costs in broadband switching and optical networks (*Source*: Annual report 2001/2002, p. 13). (See Figure 7-17.)

Changes in Accounting Policy—Fiscal Year 2002

For the fiscal year ending March 31, 2002, Marconi changed some accounting policies and reported consolidated profit and loss account with restated financial figures for 2001. The main items are shown in Figure 7-18. The income statement and balance sheet are presented according to British accounting standards.

Note the significant operating loss of £6,293 million that was mainly caused by operating exceptional items of £5,210 million in

Figure 7-16. Marconi R&D expenses.

(*£millions*)	**Fiscal year ended**	
	March 31, 2001	**March 31, 2000**
Communications networks	472	308

Figure 7-17. Marconi—key ratios.

	2000	2001	Year 2001
Operating income or loss/revenues	−7	0	Poor
Debt ratio (total debt/total assets)	59%	61%	Average
Current ratio (current assets/current liabilities)	0.93	1.31	Average
Accounts receivable days	—	109	Compare with the industry average

(See the definition of key ratios in Subchapter 4.5.)

Figure 7-18. Marconi—income statement.

£million	2002	2001 Restated
Turnover	4,310	6,653
Operating (loss)/profit	−6,293	57
Retained loss for the fiscal year	−5,875	−435

2002. Retained loss for the fiscal year rose to £5,875 million in 2002 from £435 million in 2001. Note that before the restatement of accounting, Marconi reported a net income of £180 million for 2001. The change in accounting policy affected results. (See Figure 7-19 on page 198.)

The significant loss substantially decreased shareholders' equity, which turned negative in 2002. Because of the negative shareholders' equity, Marconi ended financial restructuring with banks and bondholders. (See Subchapter 1.2 for warning flags—financial figures.)

Legal Proceedings

Legal proceedings are reported in SEC Form 20-F.

Pay attention if there are significant legal proceedings pending. It may mean high compensation in the future.

Projections

Future

On August 28, 2002, Marconi announced a restructuring process that is likely to involve a debt-for-equity swap to decrease Marconi's indebtedness. At the same time, the company group aims to complete its restructuring by the end of January 2003. In the restructuring, Marconi Corporation has planned to take on a new role as a new holding company for the group. Instead, Marconi is expected to be "liquidated" on a solvent basis. As a result, Marconi Corporation has announced its intentions to apply for a new listing on the London Stock Exchange and to establish an ADR program on NASDAQ.

The reporting of Network Components and the U.S.-based Access activities business in North America was changed to be a part of reporting in Marconi Capital. Marconi announced continued rational-

Figure 7-19. Marconi—restatement.

Group

£million	2002	2001
Fixed assets	1,649	7,128
Current assets	3,406	4,914
Net current (liabilities)/assets	−662	994
Net (liabilities)/assets after retirement benefit		
Surpluses and benefits	−1546	4,954
Equity shareholders' interests	−1558	4,939
Equity minority interests	12	15
	−1546	4,954

ization, resulting in a reduced head count, production, supply chain, and the outsourcing of manufacturing of noncomplex products.

Appendixes

Subsidiaries

Communications

Marconi Communications Ltd (U.K.)

Marconi Communications S.p.A. (Italy)

Marconi Communications North America Inc. (U.S.)

Marconi Communications, Inc. (U.S.)

Marconi Mobile S.p.A. (Italy)

Systems

Marconi Systems Holdings Inc. (U.S.)

Marconi Medical Systems, Inc. (U.S.)

Marconi Data Systems, Inc. (U.S.)

Other

Global Air Movement Holdings Limited (U.K.) (42 percent)

Marconi Applied Technologies Limited (U.K.)

Marconi Software Solutions Limited (U.K.)

Marconi Commerce Systems Inc. (U.S.)

Ipsaris Limited (U.K.) (92 percent)

General Domestic Appliances Limited (U.K.) (50 percent)

Plessey Holdings Limited (U.K.) (50 percent)

Larger companies almost always have several divisions and subsidiaries. If you are dealing with a 100 percent–owned subsidiary, it is recommended to use the financial information of the parent company in the analysis. The parent company has full financial control of its 100 percent–owned subsidiary; therefore, funding, internal pricing, and other internal transactions are possible, which affects the result of the subsidiary.

Selected Acquisitions:

Fiscal 2003
Merloni, March 2002, GDA (50 percent)

Fiscal 2002
Danaher Corp., February 2002, commerce and data systems
Royal Philips Electronics, October 2001, medical systems

Fiscal 2001
Metapath Software International (MSI), a Delaware company headquartered in London, England, providing software and services used in the wireless telecommunications market to launch and support mobile voice and data services

Fiscal 2000
Reltec: A U.S.-based company providing telecommunications access, power, and outside plant products and services
Fore Systems: A U.S.-based company providing broadband switches
Nokia's equipment transmission business
Bosch's public networks business

Several large acquisitions in a short period of time may mean difficulties in combining the new businesses organizationally. In an acquisition, good personnel may leave the company or internal disputes are possible. Internal confusion may mean inaccurate deliveries to you and additional administrative, selling, and general costs on the income statement. The price paid for the acquired company is possibly found to be too high, and thus resulting in write-

downs of goodwill on the income statement. Costs and write-downs decrease profit on the income statement.

Selected disposals
Fiscal 2003
Bookham Technology, March 2002, Marconi Optical Compo-
nents' 9.9 percent stake in Bookham Technology.

Fiscal 2002
Medical systems business was sold to Philips Electronics for ap-
proximately £780 million ($1.1 billion) in cash.
Easynet Group, July 2001, Ipsaris's 71.9 percent stake in Easynet
(49.9 percent voting rights).
SEC Form-20, pp. 21, 52.
Marconi is selling its assets by decreasing indebtedness.
*You should be aware of the possibility that the part of a company you
are interested in is included in the disposal list. The part of the com-
pany that is sold may find an even better parent company in the future.*

Sources of information:
SEC filings: Form 20-F Marconi PLC and Marconi Corpora-
tion PLC, for the fiscal year ending March 31, 2001. SEC
Form 20-F.
Marconi Web site: www.marconi.com.
August 28, 2002, Marconi PLC Statement Press Comment.

Appendix

For More Information

App. 1 Useful Sources of Information for Analyzing Suppliers

This appendix provides a large number of information sources for support in analyzing suppliers. Nowadays, there is no shortage of information. Therefore, to save time, it is important to choose the best information sources. Many of the sources listed here can be accessed through the Internet and some without any fees. Today, virtually all major information providers and companies have Web sites, so it is easy to contact them and find information.

The information sources are organized into lists. The first sources presented are free of charge, followed by the most common sources for credit information and other information.

App. 2 Free-of-Charge Information

1. *Search engines.* You can search for different types of information by company name through search engines or, for example, on the company's Web site.
Yahoo: http://www.yahoo.com
Google: http://www.google.com
AltaVista: http://www.altavista.com

2. *Stock exchanges.* Information about the stock exchange, listing requirements, and also information about the companies listed in the stock exchange.

London: http://www.londonstockexchange.com
Euronext Paris: http://www.bourse-deparis.fr/defaultgb.htm
Frankfurt Stock Exchange (Deutsche Börse AG): http://deutsche-boerse.com
Madrid Stock Exchange (Bolsa de Madrid): http://www.bolsamadrid.es/esp/portada.htm
Italian Exchange (Borsa Italiana): http://www.borsaitalia.it
New York Stock Exchange (NYSE): http://www.nyse.com
NASDAQ: http://www.nasdaq.com
Toronto Stock Exchange (TSX group): http://www.tse.com
Sao Paulo Stock Exchange (BOVESPA): http://www.bovespa.com.br/indexi.htm
Mexican Stock Exchange (Bolsa Mexicana de Valores): http://www.bmv.com.mx/bmving/index.html
Tokyo Stock Exchange: http://www.tse.or.jp
Taiwan: http://www.tse.com.tw/docs1
Singapore Exchange Ltd: http://www.ses.com.sg
Shanghai Stock Exchange (in Chinese): http://www.sse.com.cn

3. *News*
Yahoo finance: http://quote.yahoo.com
Yahoo!Finance: Information about investing in today's markets, stock research, financial news, education, mutual funds, bonds, options, community, and international.

CNN Money News

CNNmoney (money.cnn.com)

App. 3 Credit-Rating Agencies

Financial-rating agencies assess the likelihood that a company is able to fulfill its promises such as its ability to repay financial obligations to debt investors and other creditors. These ratings are called *credit ratings*. These independent rating agencies provide their services through publications and ratings advisories that are published for investors. For example, Moody's, Standard & Poor's, Fitch, and Mikuni offer credit ratings.

The ratings can be based on both quantitative and qualitative assessments of the company. The financial performance ratings are based more on a quantitative assessment of a company. The ratings are normally revised every twelve months or when something unexpected happens to the company. The scope of the analysis covers all or some of the following components: financial strength, operating performance, market profile, industry analysis, business position, management, corporate strategy, investments, capitalization, and liquidity.

Fitch is a leader in the ratings of small- to medium-size companies, while Moody's and Standard & Poor's are more focused on large companies. Mikuni's rating is specialized for Japanese companies.

The ratings give you an idea about which companies must pay higher prices for their debts. An investment-grade rating guarantees lower interest margins and a speculative grade increases the interest a company has to pay.

Moody's Investors Service

Moody's Investors Service (New York, NY) provides ratings of bond issues and company information. (See Figure App.-1.)
Web site: www.moodys.com

Figure App.-1. Moody's rating definitions.

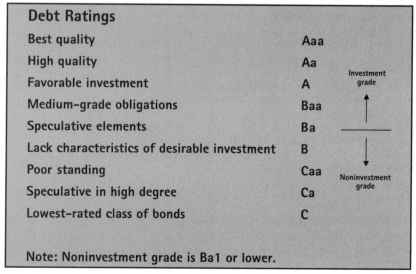

Debt Ratings		
Best quality	Aaa	
High quality	Aa	
Favorable investment	A	Investment grade
Medium-grade obligations	Baa	
Speculative elements	Ba	
Lack characteristics of desirable investment	B	
Poor standing	Caa	Noninvestment grade
Speculative in high degree	Ca	
Lowest-rated class of bonds	C	

Note: Noninvestment grade is Ba1 or lower.

Standard & Poor's Corporation (New York, NY) publishes annual services. (See Figure App.-2.)
Web site: http://www.standardandpoors.com

Fitch Ratings

Fitch Ratings research is provided through a Bloomberg terminal. There are summary research and ratings by subscription and additional Fitch Ratings services available to Bloomberg users.
Web site: http://www.fitchratings.com

Mikuni Ratings

Mikuni ratings cover long-term debt ratings and short-term note rating. The coverage of Mikuni's credit ratings is a credit-rating service of Japanese corporations. (See Figures App.-3 and App.-4.)
Web site: http://www-mikuni-rating.co.jp/eng/bond.html

Figure App.-2. Standard & Poor's ratings.

Long-term issue credit ratings		
Highest rating	AAA	
High quality	AA	Investment grade
Favorable investment	A	
Adequate protection parametres	BBB	
Less vulnerable to nonpayment than other speculative issues	BB	
Vulnerable to nonpayment than obligations rated BB	B	Noninvestment grade
Vulnerable to nonpayment	CCC	
Highly vulnerable to nonpayment	CC	
Very vulnerable to nonpayment	C	
Payment default	D	
+/– shows relative standing of rating categories.		
Note: Noninvestment grade is BB+ and lower.		

Figure App.-3. Mikuni's short-term note rating.

• M-1	• Highest standard of investment safety.
• M-2	• High standard.
• M-3	• Good standard.
• M-4	• Medium standard.
• M-5	• Lower medium standard.
• M-6	• Speculative standard.
• M-D	• Extremely speculative standard. Court protection from creditors under the procedures has been filed.

• *Source:* http://www.mikuni-rating.co.jp/eng/bond.html

Figure App.-4. Mikuni's bond & long-term debt-rating classification.

• AAA (Triple A)	• Highest standard of investment safety.
• AA (Double A)	• High standard.
• A (Single A)	• Good standard.
• BBB (Triple B)	• Medium standard.
• BB (Double B)	• Lower medium standard.
• B (Single B)	• Speculative standard.
• CCC (Triple C)	• Highly speculative standard.
• CC (Double C)	• Extremely speculative standard. Capacity to pay interest and principal is highly inadequate.
• DDD (Triple D)	• Extremely speculative standard. Court protection from creditors under the procedures has been filed.

• *Source:* http://www.mikuni-rating.co.jp/eng/bond.html

Dun & Bradstreet

Dun & Bradstreet (Bethlehem, PA) has the following services: global coverage of business information and a wide variety of publications. Web site: http://www.dnb.com

Asiakastieto (Helsinki, Finland)

Suomen Asiakastieto Oy, the Finnish-based credit information company, provides credit information in Finland about Finnish companies and companies outside of Finland. Web site: http://www.asiakastieto.com

TSR Tokyo Shoko Research, Ltd.

TSR provides credit reports in Japanese and English. The Japanese services include business information reports, data services, information services through the Internet, and business failure news. Tokyo Shoko Research, Ltd. provides two types of credit reports in English: Dun & Bradstreet reports and TSR translation reports. Web site: http://www.tsr-net.co.jp

Sinotrust Credit Information and Credit Management Services

Sinotrust is a Chinese-based company specializing in enterprise credit information and credit management services in China. Web site: http://chinafeedonline.com

Kroll

Kroll is a risk consultancy company with global solutions, such as investigation intelligence. Web site: http://www.krollworldwide.com

App. 4 Online Services

Several companies are offering news and company information in online services. Some well-known companies are listed next.

Bloomberg News

Bloomberg News (New York, NY) offers real-time, global news services that provide information on the world's governments, corporations, industries, commodities, and most segments of financial markets. The service is available on dedicated computer terminals. Bloomberg also offers online services in tabular and/or graph form. For example, Bloomberg provides the following information: financial news about industries and companies, debt ratings from several credit institutions, EDGAR filings, company analysis (from Hoover's), equity, debt, commodities, foreign exchange, and municipal market data. Bloomberg thoroughly covers the information for business needs.

Reuters

Reuters offers news and products, such as Reuters Credit, which allows a search by issuer type, industry sector, geography, rating quality, debt type, and currency information.
Web site: http://reuters.com

Financial Times

Financial Times provides news and other services such as Financial Times Online Annual Reports. FT Corporate Solutions provides products and services for businesses.
Web site: http://www.ft.com/corporate

Yahoo SmartMoney

Yahoo! Finance provides news about companies, investing, savings, and personal finance.
Web site: finance.yahoo.com

EBN

In print and online, EBN delivers the news, analysis, and in-depth reporting of the business strategies and technology trends the electronics industry needs to develop, manage, and execute successful procurement, technology, business, and supply network strategies.
Web site: http://www.ebnews.com

App. 5 Banks—Brokerage Reports

Banks and brokerage firms dealing with stock provide brokerage reports to their customers to help them in the decision-making process of buying and selling stock. Brokerage reports are written by security analysts. Several banks offer broker reports, but some of the more well-known banks include:

Morgan Stanley: http://www.morganstanley.com

JPMorgan: http://jpmorgan.com

Bank of America: http//www.bankofamerica.com

App. 6 Company Information

Financial information is normally included on a Web site in the investors' section if the company is publicly owned. If the company is privately owned, you normally must ask for the information directly from the company. The company may decline to provide the information.

A. Company Reports

The best source of company information is the company itself. Almost all companies, publicly listed or privately held, publish press releases on various subjects such as changes in management, mergers and acquisitions, financial information, and product information on their Web pages.

B. Annual Report

The annual report has been the most important source of information about a company. It provides information on current operations and financial conditions of the company. The annual report provides financial statements and information about the business operations, and the CEO's review about the future.

C. SEC Filings

Securities and Exchange Commission (SEC) files are available via Bloomberg in EDGAR files, or some companies have access to their SEC filings on their Web sites. In accordance with the Securities and Exchange Commission Act of 1934, all companies that have publicly issued securities must file various statements with the SEC and also distribute them to the stockholders.

❏ Form 10-K includes the annual report and presents the company's business and financial information in great detail. The annual reports are audited and delivered annually.

❏ Form 10-Q and quarterly reports are unaudited. Form 10-Q is filed with the SEC on a quarterly basis and should be filed within forty-five days from the end of the fiscal year. The requirements of the contents of the quarterly report include the operations for the quarter, year-to-date, and comparison with the corresponding quarter of the previous year. The report must contain an income statement, balance sheet, and funds flow statement, as well as a written analysis of the operations during the quarter.

❏ The proxy statement discloses information relevant to the stockholders.

❏ Form 8-K is an interim report filed when there is an important event that affects the corporation, such as bankruptcy, changes in control, and registration of officers or directors.

EDGAR Database

EDGAR, the electronic data-gathering, analysis, and retrieval system, is the source that provides information about U.S. SEC data. Web site: http://edgar-online.com

D. Other Sources

Companies House

This source provides company information in the United Kingdom. Web site: http://ws3info.companieshouse.gov.uk/info/

Hoover's Handbook

This handbook provides information on 500 of the largest and most influential companies in the United States. It is available through LEXIS, Bloomberg, and American Online. Profiles on the 500 companies are presented based on revenues and include an overview, history, key competitors, products and services, brand names, key personnel, and five years of financial and stock information. Web site: http://www.hoovers.com

Japan Company Handbook

The Japanese handbook has two publications: the first section and the second section. *Japan Company Handbook* is published quarterly and provides detailed information on more than 3,500 Japanese leading companies:

1. *First section.* The first section includes all the blue chip companies listed on the three major stock exchanges in Japan. The first section covers over 1,500 companies listed on the stock exchanges in Japan.

2. *Second section.* The second section includes smaller companies that are publicly listed on the stock exchange.

Web site: http://www.toyokeizai.co.jp/english/jch

Glossary

accelerated depreciation—Any depreciation that produces larger deductions for depreciation at an earlier period in a project's life cycle.

accounting period—The length of time covered by a statement of income. One year is the accounting period for most financial reporting; publicly listed companies prepare financial statements for each quarter of the year and also for each month.

accounts payable (trade payables)—Money owed to creditors for items or services purchased from them.

accounts receivable (trade credit)—Money owed by customers, or the balance sheet account that measures the amount of outstanding receivables.

acid-test ratio—A ratio that measures the liquidity of short-term assets and also shows the efficiency of the company in managing assets.

acquisition—The purchase of one enterprise by another enterprise.

additional paid-in capital—The amount by which the original sales price of stock shares sold exceeds the par value of the stock.

adverse opinion—Opinion given by an independent auditor stating the financial statements. An adverse opinion reflects that the financial statements have not been presented fairly in accordance with generally accepted accounting principles (GAAP).

allocated costs—Costs systematically assigned or distributed among products, departments, or other elements.

allowance for doubtful accounts—Related to accounts receivable and the estimated amount of collection losses.

amortization—The process of expense allocation of intangible assets.

annual report—A document issued annually by publicly owned corporations to their stockholders. Includes audited financial statements with notes for several years, as well as business information about a company and its operations.

assets—The economic resources a company possesses.

assets turnover ratio—A measure of assets efficiency defined as net sales divided by total assets.

audit—The investigation performed by an auditor. The audit can be a financial audit or a quality audit.

auditing—The act of performing an audit, enabling the auditors to express an opinion of the entity in the specific scope of the audit.

auditors—The professionals who perform audits and whose main duty is to make an auditing report in which they express their opinions.

auditors' report—The professional opinion of auditors as to the fairness of the financial statements.

average collection days—Measurement of how many days on average the accounts receivable average takes to collect. (The formula is presented in Chapter 4.5.)

balance sheet—The financial document showing the financial position of a company at a specific date. The balance sheet has two sides: assets, and liabilities and shareholders' equity. It is a document belonging to the financial statements.

bankruptcy—A legal condition in which an individual or a company's assets are used to pay off creditors.

bond—Long-term publicly issued debt.

bond rating—An appraisal by a recognized financial organization of the soundness of a bond as an investment.

book value—The value of a share based on the balance sheet values. Compare with market value.

book value of equity—The value of shareholders' equity as shown on a company's balance sheet.

break-even analysis—Analysis of the level of sales at which a company or product will just break even.

break-even point—The level of activity at which the fixed costs of an operation are barely covered by the contribution from sales. At this point, neither a profit nor a loss ensues.

bullet—A single payment of the total amount of a loan at the end of the period (as opposed to periodic payments during its life).

business risk—Risk that stems from uncertainty about investment outlays, operating cash flows, and the uncertainty of how investments are financed.

capital—The amount invested in a venture.

capital employed—The total of the long-term funds in a balance sheet. It includes shareholders' equity, long-term loans, preference shares, minority interests, and miscellaneous long-term funds. It can also be expressed as total assets minus current liabilities.

capitalization—The sum of all long-term sources of financing to a company, or the total assets.

capital market—The financial market for long-term securities.

capital stock—The transferable stocks in a corporation.

capital structure—The mixture of equity, debt funding, and retained earnings.

cash cow—A company or product that generates more cash than can be productively reinvested.

cash equivalents—Those security investments that are easily converted to cash.

cash flow cycle—The period taken to convert cash through working capital and fixed assets back to cash.

cash flow forecast—A financial forecast in the form of a source and use statement.

cash flow from financing activities—The part on a statement of cash flows showing the cash generated from or used by investing activities over a period of time.

cash flow from investing activities—The part on a statement of cash flows showing the cash spent on or received from investing activities.

cash flow from operating activities—The part on a statement of cash flows showing the cash retained from or consumed by operating activities.

cash flows—The amount of cash generated or consumed by an activity over a certain period of time. An expression describing both cash receipts (inflows) and cash payments (outflows) minus current liabilities.

cash flow statement—A report of a company's sources of cash and the uses of the cash over an accounting period.

certified public accountant (CPA)—An independent professional accountant licensed by a state to offer auditing and other accounting services to clients.

Chapter 11—A method of resolving bankruptcy that provides for reorganization of the failed company as an alternative to liquidating it. A company can file a petition for voluntary reorganization on its own behalf or an outside party, usually a creditor, initiates involuntary reorganization.

collateral—A physical or financial asset used as security for a loan.

collection period—A ratio measure of control of accounts receivable defined as accounts receivable divided by credit sales per day. (See Chapter 4.5.)

common share/common stock—Common stock securities representing ownership rights including the right to vote.

comparative financial statement—Financial statement figures of two or more years, presented side by side.

competence—The knowledge and skills an individual brings to a company to achieve a goal or perform a task.

consolidated financial statements—Financial statements that show the combined activities of a parent company and its subsidiaries. The combination consists of two or more separate legal entities. The parent company owns more than 50 percent of the voting stock of one of the companies.

convertible security—Financial security that can be exchanged at the holder's option for another security or assets.

core—The vital part of a business.

corporate restructuring—Any major change in a company's internal structure or ownership structure.

cost of goods sold—The cost of the inventory items sold during the period.

cost of sales—The sum of all costs required to acquire and prepare goods for sale.

coverage ratio—The measure of financial leverage relating annual operating income to annual burden of debt.

creative accounting—An accounting with extended accounting principles.

creditor—A lender to which money is owed.

credit rating—Given by credit rating agencies such as Moody's and Standard & Poor's after evaluating credit worthiness of businesses.

current asset—Any asset that will be converted into cash within one year.

current liability—Any liability that is payable within one year.

current portion of long-term debt—The portion of long-term debt that is payable within one year.

current ratio—A measure of liquidity defined as current assets divided by current liabilities.

debt capacity—The total amount of debt a company can prudently support, given its earnings expectations and equity base.

debt (liability)—An obligation to pay cash or other goods or to provide services to another.

debt-to-assets ratio—A measure of financial leverage defined as debt divided by total assets.

debt-to-equity ratio—A measure of financial leverage defined as debt divided by shareholders' equity.

default—To fail to make a payment when due.

depreciation—The systematic measure of the cost of a fixed asset to expense during the periods of its useful lifetime.

dividend—The amount a company pays to its shareholders from its retained earnings.

earnings before interest and taxes (EBIT)—The operating profit of a company.

earnings before interest, taxes, depreciation, and amortization (EBITDA)—The profit after several items.

earnings per common share—The net earnings for the period divided by the average number of common stock shares outstanding.

expenses—The cost of the goods and services used for obtaining revenue.

FASB (Financial Accounting Standards Board)—The entity currently responsible for developing U.S. generally accepted accounting principles (GAAP). *See also* **GAAP.**

financial audit—A thorough investigation of a company's financial statements by an independent auditor.

financial gearing—The measures of the relative amount of debt to equity in a company's balance sheet. More commonly used in the United Kingdom. A company is said to be highly geared when debts exceed equity in the capital structure.

financial leverage—The level at which a company uses debt financing. More commonly used in the United States.

financial position—The balance sheet shows the financial resources and obligations of a company at one point in time.

financial ratios—Calculations made to analyze and compare financial data.

financial reporting—The process of periodically providing financial information.

financial statements—The four different financial accounting reports that concisely summarize the results of a company's operations and current financial position of the company.

fiscal year—A twelve-month accounting period in a business.

fixed assets—Tangible, long-lived assets intended for use to generate wealth rather than being held for resale. Those assets are expected to provide a service benefit for more than one year.

fixed costs—Costs not dependent on sales. (*See* **variable costs.**)

focus business—The business that a company is or will be focused on in the future.

focused approach—The key message in the focused approach is the direct impact of competitive position and market value of a company.

focused enterprise—A company that is primarily focused on producing one or a small number of products and services in-house.

Form 10-K—An annual document filed with the Securities and Exchange Commission (SEC) by publicly listed companies in the United States.

GAAP (Generally Accepted Accounting Principles)—Accounting concepts, measurement techniques, rules, and standards of presentation used in financial statements. The Financial Accounting Standards Board is the body that is responsible for GAAP. *See also* **FASB.**

gearing—An expression of the debt-to-equity ratio. A relationship between different types of funds in a company, such as loans and equity.

goodwill—Intangible assets appear in the financial statements only if the company is acquired for a price in excess of the fair market value of its net assets.

highly geared—A company is called highly geared when debt exceeds equity in its capital structure. The more highly geared that a company is, the more vulnerable it is to takeovers and bankruptcy.

income statement (statement of income)—A financial statement showing the results of operations of a business over a period of time, usually a year (U.S. term).

initial public offering (IPO)—The admission of a company's share in a stock exchange, when the company comes to a market.

intangible assets—Items such as licenses and patents that have no physical characteristics but create value for a company.

interest coverage—A liquidity ratio showing the number of times interest expenses on the income statement can be paid by free cash flows.

interim statement—Financial statements issued quarterly or semiannually for periods shorter than one year.

International Accounting Standards (IAS)—A set of global accounting standards.

International Accounting Standards Board (IASB)—A board to develop a single set of global accounting standards. IASB replaced the International Accounting Standard Committee (IASC).

inventories—Items for commercial purposes held for sale or used in the manufacturing of products.

inventory turnover (stock turnover ratio)—A ratio reflecting how many times a company's inventory turns per year. (See Chapter 4.5.)

issued share capital—The authorized share capital that has been issued to shareholders.

keiretsu—Interrelated companies around a major bank or industrial enterprise in Japan.

leverage ratio—A ratio that measures the extent of a company's financing with debt relative to equity.

liabilities—A company's debts or obligations and claims of creditors.

liquidity—The ability of a company to generate sufficient cash to meet requirements.

liquidity ratio—A ratio that measures a company's ability to meet needs for cash requirements as they arise.

long-term debt—Obligations with maturities beyond one year.

market value—The current price of marketable assets in market. Market value and book value can be the same if there is no difference between the purchase price and market price, less accumulated depreciation. Generally, market value and book value are different. Compare with book value.

matching principle—The goal is to offset a reasonable portion of the asset's cost against revenue in each period of the asset's useful life. (*See* **depreciation**.)

merger—In a merger, two different enterprises are consolidated into a single enterprise.

minority interest—The claims of shareholders other than the parent company's claims of its subsidiary.

mortgage—A debt instrument granting conditional ownership of an asset that is secured by the asset.

multiple sources—More suppliers with more locations to deal with a specific product or service.

NASDAQ (National Association of Securities Dealers Automated Quotation)—This telecommunications network of dealers provides current bidding and asking prices on thousands of actively traded over-the-counter securities.

net assets—The difference between total assets minus total liabilities.

net earnings—A company's profit or loss after all revenue and expenses reported during the accounting period.

net income—The amount of increase in owners' equity resulting from profitable operations.

net loss—The amount of decrease in owners' equity resulting from unprofitable operations.

net sales—Total sales revenue less those items corrected in the sales, such as sales returns and sales allowances.

nonconsolidated financial statements—Financial statements of a single enterprise.

noncurrent assets/liabilities—Items expected to benefit a company with maturities beyond a period of one year.

notes to the financial statement—Additional information to financial statements explaining a company's accounting policies and providing details about particular accounts. Notes are an essential part to explain the financial statements.

off balance sheet financing—Liabilities that do not show on the balance sheet; financial special techniques for raising funds.

operating expenses—Costs accrued in the course of normal business functions.

operating income (operating profit)—Sales revenue less the expenses from generating sales. Operating income measures the overall profitability of a company's normal, ongoing operations.

outsourcing—A company has made a strategic decision not to execute the task itself and instead will have another company provide the service or produce the product for the company.

over-the-counter exchange (OTC)—An intangible market for the purchase and sale of securities not listed by the organized exchanges.

overtrading—An expression indicating that if a company expands too rapidly, it might fail.

owners' equity (shareholders' equity)—Assets minus liabilities; the amount of the owners' investment in a business, including profits or losses from business operations.

paid-in capital—The amount the investors have invested in a company.

parent company—A company that owns wholly or partly (normally over 50 percent) the shares of another company (termed *subsidiaries*).

partnership—An unincorporated business owned by two or more persons voluntarily acting as partners (co-owners).

preferred stock—The capital stock of a company that gives preferences over the other stock, for example, in dividends and in the distribution of assets in the event of liquidation.

prepaid expenses—Expenditures made in the current or previous period that will benefit a company.

profitability—The profitable business that operations generate increases the owners' equity.

profit and loss statement (statement of income)—The profit and loss statement reflects the revenues and costs in the period. It is a document in the financial statements.

pro forma financial statements—Projections of future financial statements based on a set of assumptions. Pro forma numbers strip the negative items from the income statements. These income statements came into use during the dot-com years.

prospectus—A documented, written description of a mutual fund required by the Securities and Exchange Commission.

public information—Something that is available to the general public.

publicly owned corporations, publicly held companies—Corporations in which shares are traded publicly.

public offering—New securities are made available for sale to the general public.

purchasing—The acquisition of goods or services in return for equivalent payment (*see* **sourcing**).

qualified opinion—An opinion given by an independent auditor when the overall financial statements are fairly presented "except for" certain items (disclosed by the auditor).

quality of financial reporting—A subjective evaluation of the extent to which financial reporting accurately reflects the financial condition and operating success of a company.

quick assets—The most liquid current assets: includes only cash, marketable securities, and receivables.

quick ratio (acid test)—A measure of short-term debt-paying ability. Quick assets are termed *current assets divided by current liabilities*. Quick ratio takes into account only the most liquid assets.

raw materials—Basic commodities or natural resources that will be used in the production of goods.

restructuring charges—Costs caused by reorganizing a company.

results of operations—A description of a company's financial activities during the year.

retained earnings—The amount of the owners' equity in a corporation that has accumulated as a result of profitable business operations. Retained earnings are not cash, but rather have been utilized to finance the company's assets.

return on assets (ROA)—A measure of the efficiency with which management utilizes the assets of a business. (See Chapter 4.5.)

return on equity (ROE)—The percentage return gained by a company for the equity shareholders.

return on investment (ROI)—Net profit divided by assets, expressed as a percentage.

return on total assets (ROTA)—Profit before interest and tax divided by total assets, expressed as a percentage.

revenue—The price of goods and services received from business.

risk—Risk associated with profit and the possibility of loss.

risk management—A continuous process where the risks of operations and products are analyzed systematically.

Securities and Exchange Commission (SEC)—In the United States, a body with the legal power to establish financial reporting requirements for large, publicly owned corporations.

selling and administration expenses—Costs of a company's management function to keep the company's business going.

senior debt—Debt that ranks ahead of junior, or subordinated debt, in the event of liquidation. (*See* **subordinated debt.**)

sensitivity analysis—A qualitative approach to focus upon the weaknesses of a company.

shareholders' equity—The amount the owners have invested in the business, including income retained in the business.

shareholders' funds—Includes the issued ordinary shares plus reserves plus preference shares.

short term—Maturity in a period of less than one year.

short-term loans (STL)—All liabilities due within one year: bank overdrafts, current portion of long-term debts, and other interest-bearing liabilities.

solvency—The financial ability to pay debts as they become due.

sourcing—A synonymous term for purchasing, which implies the acquisition of goods or services in return for payment. (*See* **purchasing**: used interchangeably in this book.)

start-up—A newly established company, operated in the maket less than three years.

statement of cash flows—The financial statement summarizing the cash inflows and cash outflows during an accounting period.

strategy—Divided into different levels of strategies, for example, corporate strategy, business strategy, and functional or operational strategy. Different strategies define the business and ways to compete in the selected business.

subordinated debt—Debts that have repayment after senior debt.

subsidiary—A company is a subsidiary of another company (called the parent company) if the parent company owns more than 50 percent of the equity or effectively controls the company by means of voting shares or composition of the board of directors.

supplier—The word *supplier* is used in this book to mean a company that delivers products or services. Suppliers include components suppliers, R&D suppliers, subsuppliers, and partners; all the companies that might supply the enterprise.

supplier base—All suppliers.

tangible assets—Assets with physical substance—for example, plant and machinery or motor vehicles.

tax rate—The rate of tax on profit.

times interest earned—The measure of the coverage of debt. (See Chapter 4.5.)

total assets—The summary of all assets (fixed assets, intangible assets, and current assets), and all liabilities (current liabilities and long-term liabilities and other liabilities) and owners' equity.

treasury stock—Shares of a corporation that have been repurchased by the corporation.

trend analysis—An analysis of financial data over several accounting periods.

unqualified opinion—The financial statement that an independent auditor has stated to present a fair presentation, in accordance with generally accepted accounting principles.

useful life—The time span over which the depreciable asset is expected to be useful to the business.

variable costs—Costs that vary according to the volume of the business activity.

wide-range approach—Also called the traditional approach, it represents a company that does not have any specific focus area or has several focus areas. The company internally produces the services and products it needs to manufacture the end products.

wide-range enterprise—A company that produces services and products internally within the company.

working capital—A measure of short-term debt-paying ability. Working capital is calculated as follows: current assets minus current liabilities.

work-in-process—Products in the manufacturing process that are not fully completed, for example, materials costs, variable wages, and salaries.

write-down—The revaluation of inventory when the current value is lower than the book value at which the inventory is carried. Write-downs that are too small or too big enable companies to manipulate their results.

write-off—An accounting process in which slow-moving or worthless inventory is removed from the books. A write-off adds to costs in statements of income. The term *write-off* is used to refer to bad debts that have to be written off similarly to goodwill. Bad debts, those debts that a customer is unable to pay, normally due to bankruptcy, are written off against the provision for bad debts account.

Bibliography

Books

Atrill, Peter, and Eddie McLaney. *Accounting and Finance for Nonspecialist,* 2nd ed. Badmin, Cornwall, Great Britain: Prentice-Hall, 1996.

Beaver, William H., and George Paker. *Risk Management: Problems & Solutions.* New York: McGraw Hill, 1995.

Bowman, Cliff. *Strategy in Practice.* Harlow, England: Prentice Hall Europe, 1998.

Brannen, Christalyn, and Tracey Wilen. *Doing Business with Japanese Men: A Woman's Handbook.* Berkeley, Calif.: Stone Bridge Press, 1993.

Brealey, Richard A., and Stewart C. Myers. *Principles of Corporate Finance,* 4th ed. New York: McGraw-Hill, 1991.

Caouette, John B., Edward I. Altman, and Paul Narayanan. *Managing Credit Risk: The Next Great Financial Challenge.* New York: John Wiley & Sons, 1998.

Chopra, Sunil, and Peter Meindl. *Supply Chain Management, Strategy, Planning, and Operation.* Paramus, New Jersey: Prentice-Hall, 2001.

Delaney, Patrick R., Barry J. Epstein, Ralph Nach, and Susan Weiss Budak. *GAAP 2002, Interpresentation and Application of Generally Accepted Accounting Principles 2002.* New York: John Wiley & Sons, 2001.

Fitch, Thomas P. *Dictionary of Banking Terms,* 3rd ed. Hauppauge, New York: Barron's, 1997.

Fridson, Martin S. *Financial Statement Analysis: A Practitioner's Guide.* New York: John Wiley & Sons, 1991.

Fukuda, Shigeyoshi, Mariko Mitsubori, and Yasuko Machida. *Nippon: The*

Land and Its People. Japan: Nippon Steel Human Resource Development, 1997.

Grey, Stephen. *Practical Risk Assessment for Project Management.* New York: John Wiley & Sons, 1998.

Hammel, Gary. *Leading the Revolution.* Boston: Harvard Business School Press, 2000.

Harrison, Walter T., Jr., and Charles T. Horngren. *Financial Accounting,* 3rd ed. Paramus, New Jersey: Prentice-Hall, 1998.

Higgins, Robert C. *Analysis for Financial Management,* 3rd ed. Ill.: Irwin Professional Publishing, 1992.

Hingley, Wifred. *Accounting.* Bungay, Suffolk: Made Simple Books, 1989.

Katayama, Patricia, Hisako Nosaki Ifshin, and Kirsten Rocelle McIvor. *Talking about Japan—Q&A.* Tokyo, Japan: Kodansha International, 1996.

Kester, W. Carl. *Japanese Takeovers: The Global Contest for Corporate Control.* Boston: Harvard Business School Press, 1991.

King, Thomas E., Valdean C. Lembke, and John H. Smith. *Financial Accounting: A Decision-Making Approach.* New York: John Wiley & Sons, 1997.

Kontio, Jyrki. *Software Engineering Risk Management: A Method, Improvement Framework, and Empirical Evaluation* (doctoral dissertation). Suomen Laatukeskus. Helsinki, Finland: Helsinki University of Technology, Center for Excellence, 2001.

Lerner, Josh. *Venture Capital and Private Equity: A Casebook.* New York: John Wiley & Sons, 2000.

Lewis, Jordan D. *The Connected Corporation: How Leading Companies Win Through Customer-Supplier Alliances.* New York: The Free Press, 1995.

Lysons, Kenneth. *Purchasing and Supply Chain Management.* London: Pearson Education Limited, 2000.

Meigs, Walter B., Mary A. Meigs, and Robert F. Meigs. *Financial Accounting.* New York: McGraw-Hill, 1995.

Mikel, Harry, and Richard Schroeder. *Six Sigma: The Breakthrough Management Strategy Revolutionizing the World's Top Corporations.* New York: Doubleday, 2000.

Moore, Geoffrey A. *Inside the Tornado.* New York: HarperCollins, 1995.

Moore, Geoffrey A. *Crossing the Chasm.* New York: HarperCollins, 1999.

Moore, Geoffrey A. *Living on the Fault Line.* New York: HarperCollins, 2000.

Naumann, Earl, and Steven H. Hoisington. *Customer Centered Six Sigma: Linking Customers, Process Improvement, and Financial Results.* American Society for Quality, 2000.

Nobes, Christopher, and Robert Paker. *Comparative International Accounting.* New York: Prentice-Hall, 1995.

Porter, Michael E. *Competitive Strategy: Techniques for Analyzing Industries and Competitors.* New York: Free Press, 1998.

Sneyd, Peter. *Principles of Accounting and Finance.* London: Routledge, 1994.

Vaughan, Emmett J. *Risk Management.* New York: John Wiley & Sons, 1997.

Wald, J. *Bigg's Cost Accounts.* Singapore: Pitman Publishing, 1984.

Walsh, Ciaran. *Key Management Ratios: How to Analyze, Compare and Control the Figures That Drive Company Value.* Glasgow: Prentice-Hall, 1996.

Ward, Keith. *Corporate Financial Strategy.* Butterworth-Heinemann, Avon, 2000.

White, Gerald I., Ashwinpaul C. Sondhi, and Dov Fried. *The Analysis and Use of Financial Statements,* 2nd ed. New York: John Wiley & Sons, 1997.

Whittington, Richard. *What Is Strategy—And Does It Matter?* Cornwall: Thomson Learning, 2001.

Wideman, Max R. *Project & Program Risk Management: A Guide to Managing Project Risks and Opportunities.* Newton Square, Pa.: Project Management Institute, 1992.

Young, Peter C., and Steven C. Tippins. *Managing Business Risk: An Organization-Wide Approach to Risk Management.* New York: AMACOM Books, 2001.

Articles

Boehm, B. W., "Software Risk Management: Principles and Practices," *IEEE Software,* vol. 8, no. 1, 1991, pp. 32–41.

Casabona, Patrick, and Victoria Shoaf, "International Financial Reporting Standards: Significance, Acceptance, and New Developments," *Review of Business,* winter 2002, pp. 16–18.

Cleaver, Joanne Y., "Credit Insurers: The Road Ahead," *Collections & Credit Risk,* vol. 6, no. 12, December 2001, p. 45.

Connor, Michael, "M&A Risk Management (For mergers and acquisitions to be successful, any impediments to integration must be identified and understood," *Journal of Business Strategy,* vol. 22, no. 1, January 2001, pp. 25–27.

Cooke, Sarah, Laurence Rivat, Martin Faarbour, and Paul Martin, "Accounting Standards," *International Tax Review,* vol. 12, no. 7, July 2001, pp. 10, 27.

Cruz, Elften Sicangco, "Framework: Risk Management," *Businessworld (Philippines),* March 27, 2001, p. 5.

Dey, Prasanta Kumar, "Project Risk Management: A Combined Analytical Hierarchy Process and Decision Tree Approach," *Cost Engineering,* vol. 44, no. 3, March 2002, pp. 13–14.

DiCara, Vincent, "Financial Projections: A Useful Tool for Lenders (Credit Analysis)," *Commercial Lending Review,* vol. 17, no. 2b, March 2002, p. 37.

Fordham, David R., Diane A. Riordan, and Michael P. Riordan, CPA,

"How Accountants Bring Value to the Marketing Function," *Strategic Finance*, May 2002, pp. 25–26.

Gomez, Lucas, CCE, "Enron—A Case for Better Understanding of Cash Flows," *Business Credit*, July/August 2002, pp. 12–13.

Hastings, Richard D., "Supplier Credit and Credit Networks Step Up to the Plate: The Role of Business Credit During Deteriorating Business Conditions," *Business Credit*, vol. 103, no. 10, November 2001, p. 35.

Houston, Melvin, and Alan Reinstein, "International Accounting Standards and Their Implications for Accountants and U.S. Financial Statement Users," *Review of Business*, summer 2001, pp. 75–79.

Kopp, Guillermo, "Thoroughly Modern Risk Management," *Bank Technology News*, May 2002, p. 34.

Lee, Peter, "Credit Analysts Get Back to Fundamentals," *Euromoney*, no. 396, April 2002, pp. 72, 76.

Lindow, Paul E., and Jill D. Race, "Beyond Traditional Audit Techniques," *Journal of Accountancy*, July 2002, pp. 28–33.

Maher, Matt, Diane K. Schooley, and Phil Fry, "Classroom Financial Analysis with Electronic Databases," *Journal of Education for Business*, January–February 2001, pp. 144–147.

Main, Bruce W., "Risk Assessment Is Coming: Are You Ready? Understanding the Risk Assessment Process and Its Benefits," *Professional Safety*, July 2002, pp. 32–34.

Osborn, Michele C., "Accounting Standards: Nationally or Internationally Set?" *Ohio CPA Journal*, October–December, 2001, pp. 63–64.

Pyra, Jim, and John Trask, "Risk Management Post Analysis: Gauging the Success of a Simple Strategy in a Complex Project," *Project Management Journal*, June 2002, pp. 41–42.

Radcliffe, Vaughan S., David R. Campbell, and Timothy J. Fogarty, "Exploring Downsizing: A Case Study on the Use of Accounting Information," *Journal of Management Accounting Research*, 2001, pp. 131–141.

Ranson, Brian J., "Using Models in Managing Credit-Risk Portfolios; Managing Credit-Risk Portfolios Requires Use of, and Understanding Limits of, Credit Models," *Commercial Lending Review*, vol. 16, no. 4, fall 2001, p. 6.

Ratcliffe, Thomas A., and John Stephen Grice, "Evaluating Audit Differences," *CPA Journal*, January 2002, pp. 29–35.

Reason, Tim, "On the Same Page," *CFO*, May 2002, pp. 89–92.

Tannenbaum, Bryan A., "Early Warning Signals—A Sign of Things to Come?" *Business Credit*, vol. 104, no. 1, January 2002, p. 51.

Wild, Ken, and Johan T. Smith, "GAAP Differences in Your Pocket: IAS and US GAAP," *IAS Plus Deloitte Touche Tohmatsu*, July 2002, pp. 5–19 (www.deloitte.com, www.iasplus.com, info@iasplus.com).

Zolkos, Rodd, "Companies Moving to Comprehensive Risk Management," *Business Insurance*, vol. 36, no. 17, April 2002, p. 26.

Other Material

Intel Corporation, United States Securities and Exchange Commission, Washington, D.C. 20549, Form 10-Q, June 29, 2002; and Form 10-K, for the fiscal year ending December 29, 2001

Marconi, Annual Report and Accounts, 2001/2002

Marconi, Financial Restructuring: Indicative Heads of Terms, September 6, 2002

Marconi Management Report for the year ending March 31, 2002, group overview

Marconi PLC and Marconi Corporation PLC, United States Securities and Exchange Commission, Washington, D.C., 20549, Form 20-F, September 28, 2001

Marconi PLC, 2001/2002 Preliminary Statements, Press release, London—May 16, 2002

SCI/Sanmina Corporation, United States Securities and Exchange Commission, Washington, D.C. 20549, Form 10-K, for the fiscal year ending September 29, 2001

Index

231